THE GOLDEN AGE
OF CRICKET
1890–1914

LUTTERWORTH PRESS Richard Smart Publishing

THE GOLDEN AGE
OF CRICKET
1890–1914

DAVID FRITH

Foreword by J. B. Priestley

First published 1978

Published by Lutterworth Press
Luke House, Farnham Road, Guildford, Surrey
and Richard Smart Publishing
Copyright © David Frith, 1978
Foreword copyright © J. B. Priestley, 1978
ISBN 0 7188 7022 0
Printed by Jolly & Barber Limited
Rugby, Warwickshire

Half-title photograph is
of Victor Trumper, by
George W. Beldam;
title-page photograph
is of The Parks, Oxford,
in 1894

CONTENTS

To Edward Frith,
born the day
the Aussies beat Gloucester
and the Players
beat the Gentlemen

FOREWORD

FOR some reason that is never clear to me, I am always being asked to write Forewords and Introductions. It is not, I think, that editors and publishers imagine that I am unusually wise or witty. (I am not unwise, but wit has been creeping away from my old age.) And few of them can be foolish enough to believe my name will sell a book that otherwise might be ignored. All that they can hope for is that I might add a bit of ballast to what could seem a lightish craft. But adding ballast can turn out to be coolie labour, and so can writing Forewords and Introductions. You can sweat away and end up with nothing that gives you or anybody else any pleasure.

It was David Frith's title, a very artful job, that trapped me. *The Golden Age of Cricket* – oh yes, yes, yes! I am fond of cricket, even though I never acquired much skill at it, as I flatter myself I did at soccer. But who wants a Golden Age of Soccer? Certainly I don't. It just won't carry a Golden Age, at least not to us English. It simply doesn't offer us any sunlight, green fields, bright-eyed girls in their summer dresses. All too often you were playing in the rain, or at best floundering in the mud, while all those girls were staying at home, munching chocolates and reading those romantic novels in which beautiful shopgirls married dukes and earls and then were busy rearranging the furniture in remote castles.

Even so, though Mr Frith is not writing about my own chosen game – and I was a fool not to have demanded in my teens some special coaching in cricket – his book fascinates me, and I keep taking another peep into it when I ought to be doing something else. (I am old and rather weary now, but there is always a *something else* I ought to be doing.) But then, at least to an Englishman, this is what always happens when cricket is the subject in hand. The truth is, cricket is half a game with the other half always turning up as an inexhaustible topic. I cannot believe that there is another game in the world that releases so many floods of nostalgic reminiscence. The rain, as it so often does, may be turning the pitch into a morass, with the light going at every moment, but there we sit in the pavilion, lighting our pipes, lending a willing ear to tales of other matches, where the sun shone steadily and great deeds were done.

But then cunning Mr Frith, not content simply with cricket, baits his hook with a *Golden Age*. Rather recklessly, just because other authors may take advantage of this confession, I will admit I am very much a *Golden Age* man. Bring that in, and there I am, reading away, probably with my mouth wide open. Of course most of us have our own private Golden Ages, to which we look back as if remembering a lost world. My own is roughly from 1910 to 1914, when I joined the army and began to lose so many friends, when I entered another sort of world, *which could never again be trusted*. (Nor, for that matter, would ever be able to create another Golden Age of anything, unless we include various chances to cheat the public out of tidy though dubious fortunes.) There never seemed much money about from 1910 to 1914, but then you didn't need much money and if you were young you could have a lively night out on a shilling. And if you were older and were making good money, at least you weren't taxed to hell and back. But of course it couldn't last. Golden Ages, however different in other respects, have this in common: they will soon come to an end.

However, we must return to cricket. Now here I must make an important point. Before we start denouncing this age of big money and television and Packer deals, being a truthful man, I must confess that I know a great deal more about cricket than I did when I used to play the game, so many years ago; and this is due to the fact that I have watched it so often on television, which has brought me closer to first-class batting and bowling than I ever was before, when at best I had to watch it from a too-distant pavilion. It is this admirable invention that has enabled me to observe closely those duels between talented slow bowlers and brilliant batsmen which illuminate this splendid game. There is a lot to be said for that older and quieter world that seemed to offer us more fascinating characters in our cricket, but even so, nobody who loves the game should be the first to denounce what television has been able to show him.

However, I am here to welcome Mr Frith's book and I do it knowing very well that when I ought to be doing something more useful and important – like earning a good living – in an age of inflation, soon I shall be taking his book down from its shelf, to dip into it yet again when I ought to be working. Though debt and disaster may be on the way, I halt here to welcome the book and to thank its creator.

J. B. PRIESTLEY, O.M.

INTRODUCTION

We live in reference to past experience and not to future events, however inevitable.

H. G. WELLS

TODAY there are poignantly few remnants of that era, 1890 to 1914: the faded frontages of houses grand or humble, a bridge, a statue, a war memorial, musty books, pubs, piers and pavilions – and, moving through the streets, usually unsteadily with antiquity, or gazing out through protective windows at the puzzling, abrasive new world, the diminishing ranks of men and women who were born in the reign of Victoria or of Edward the Seventh. As this book neared completion, Charlie Chaplin died – five hundred miles from Walworth, his birthplace, near Kennington Oval – and the last member of the glorious Malvern and Worcestershire brotherhood of Fosters – N J A ('Johnny') – also left us: further strands cut, leaving the old days more mirage-like across the Deserts of Time than ever.

I knew only one of my grandparents: a tired, sadfaced, pinafored old lady who sometimes hummed *Goodbye, Dolly Gray* or, in hesitant voice, sang a garbled *Soldiers of the King*, while I stamped up and down the hallway. Pervading in her last years an aroma of rheumatism ointment, she survived long enough to see the Battle of Britain but not to know of D-Day. Still seemingly more concerned about the Kaiser than Hitler, she had as her heroes, never to be replaced, Kitchener and Beatty and a small army of music-hall stars. As a young woman she had been in service in a large house in Kent, and was there – though she would not have known it, or cared if she had – in the year that Frank Woolley first played for the county: 1906. When, in 1976, I spent some stardust-scattered days in the company of Woolley, it seemed that a ring of events had joined up. Yet it was a fragile link, made of thin, over-wishful circumstance. Rhoda Jane Thomas and the age to which she belonged were long since swallowed by Time, unreachable as was her dark-haired husband, whose only surviving photograph, which used to hang in that hallway, revealed sinewy forearms, a warm smile, and a groom's care for his horse. Now even that picture is lost.

While tons of ephemera has been sacrificed through carelessness, stupidity or sheer expediency, the game of cricket has weathered the ravages of time better than many other branches of human activity. Its literature, art and relics survive in collections private and public, fascilitating a reconstruction of the attitudes and manifestations of any era from Hambledon to Packer.

Of all the phases in cricket's history none has the seductive charm of the late-Victorian and Edwardian period. The glorious designation 'Golden Age' might almost as easily be conferred upon other times: the 'Middle Ages' of 'Felix, Wenman, Hillyer, Fuller Pilch, and Alfred Mynn', or part of the between-wars period, when Hammond, Bradman, and Headley were on display, or even recent years, when skill and flair have probably been spread more thickly over the cricket-fields of all Test-playing countries than ever before – granted that at least another thirty years must pass before the 1970s are lit by the soft, romantic shafts of museum lighting.

The remoteness of the pre-First World War epoch and the recognition that, assuredly though it was to end some way or other, it *did* end abruptly and indescribably tragically – for these reasons, the players of that time (and not only the household names) are hallowed in cricket lore. They did, after all, reflect the moods of the life around them. It was a time of complacency, security and opulent pride for Britain and her splendid Empire, and the ascent of wide-girthed 'Teddy' to the throne heralded warm, succulent breezes of gaiety which dislodged and dispersed inhibitions. Notwithstanding the high rates of infant mortality, drunkenness, poverty and prostitution, and a life expectancy for men of only 46, many shared the conviction of Cecil Rhodes that the British were the world's first race, and the more of the world they inhabited the better it would be for humanity; this absorption would also ensure the end of all wars. Perhaps the man had a point.

Class distinctions held firm, in cricket as in real life, though it has long been a prime claim for English cricket that it has brought all breeds of men together in a pavilion. This it may have done, creating an additional mystique, but it could never bring about any real fusion of species. The county club professional, glad to lodge with his fellows in one-star or even starless hotels, addressed the amateur as 'Mister' or 'Sir' and answered to his Christian name or nickname if he were favoured, but more likely to his surname, though without resentment. The amateur – the 'gentleman' – came usually from public school, the yield from which, C. B. Fry once wrote, apart from being 'the most valuable product of education in Europe', had 'an apologetic gaucherie, a kind of communal symbolism in refutation of any possible accusation of "side".' He had a position in the family business, the church, one of the other professions, or, as an Australian newspaper stated of one of the English amateurs in the 1890s, 'he does nothing for a living'. The county amateurs occupied separate and usually more comfortable dressing-rooms, and took the field through a separate gate. Wilfred Rhodes, late in his long life, compared this with the apartheid of South Africa – again, without resentment.

The dissolution of clear divisions, in sport as in wider life, has been hastened by two world wars and a succession of economic and political upheavals. The workers were then still some way short of governing their own affairs, just as professional cricketers found no cause, inclination or opportunity to govern the game themselves (until the 1970s). That is not to say that all was serenity. W. G. Grace's remuneration, which made a mockery of his amateur status, provoked sharp if not widespread criticism, and in 1896 he persuaded the Surrey secretary to issue a statement on the matter before confirming his willingness to lead England in the Test match against Australia. The importance of WG's presence can be imagined. At the same time, Andrew Stoddart, one of the world's great batsmen, withdrew from the England team partly because of a heavy cold and partly because of an attack by the *Morning Leader* upon him for allegedly making money out of the game when he was supposed to be a man of independent means.

Yet the sounds of these two crises have been lost in the echoing thunder of 'The Strike'. Five of the professionals – Abel, Hayward, Lohmann, Richardson (all of Surrey), and Gunn – wrote to the Surrey secretary demanding a match fee of £20 each, double the normal amount. Lohmann and Gunn would not be moved, but the other three relented in the face of an unconciliatory committee, and joined in the glory of match and series victory.

In this year there had already been a disturbance of a different kind, though not unfamiliar to modern sports-followers. Ranjitsinhji, the noble Rajput, heir to the throne of Nawanagar, was considered by MCC to be ineligible to play for England, and had to wait until the second Test for his debut. The Lancashire authorities had no compunction in selecting him, and he rewarded them with a magical 62 and 154 not out, finishing with a trickle of blood curling down from an earlobe, the price of a rare missed hook against the Australian express bowler Ernie Jones (the same incorrigible colonial who sent a ball swishing through WG's beard).

There were other irregular goings-on. In 1890, Stoddart felt it was more important to assist Middlesex against Kent at Tonbridge than England against Australia at Lord's. He was again chosen for the second Test match, at The Oval, but preferred to play in the county match at Bradford. When Lord Hawke got wind of this he stopped two of his professionals, George Ulyett and Bobby Peel, from playing in the Test. Whatever justice there was in this may be deduced from the scoreline: Mr A. E. Stoddart c Ulyett b Peel 7 c Jackson b Peel 0. At least Stoddart played under his own name. It was not uncommon for certain amateurs to play under false names, which can hardly have helped the cricket-writers in the compiling of averages – numerical columns that, incidentally, had yet to be transformed into pagan deities, for the worship of the masses.

The seventh Lord Hawke was born in 1860, a descendant of Admiral Lord Hawke, hero of the Battle of Quiberon in 1759. Like his ancestor, he had a deep sense of consideration for his men. Yet history has treated him unkindly. He is thought of as a symbol of unapproachability, of repression, and of privilege. Autocratic as well as aristocratic he may have been, but he was a leader, and the undisciplined group of cricketers that were Yorkshire became a team under Hawke (the White Rose county won nine Championships in the twenty seasons to 1912): a team of professionals with a new set of standards as well as security unknown by their predecessors. His Lordship concerned himself with such revolutionary ideas as winter payment, talent money, and the safeguarding of benefit proceeds for a cricketer's old age. He demanded loyalty in return – and a proper code of conduct from predominantly uncultured men. So that when Peel drowned his sobriety once too often, urinating on the pitch, he was sent from the ground and from Yorkshire's payroll forever. One wonders what television news editors of today would have made of that.

The demarcation between amateur and professional cricketer was officially ended, perhaps somewhat late, on November 26, 1962, when, financially at least, all cricketers became players and equal – subsequently give or take an overseas star signing. At a stroke, the 156 years of Gentlemen *v* Players matches were sealed off and mummified. Since 1806, the best of the paid players had played the pick of the unpaid in meaningful contests which had matched fervour with delight. With the years, 'shamateurism' had become quite widespread, and so yet another anachronism was killed off. The most apt and perhaps predictable graffiti one could find today on the old walls of Lord's, The Oval, Headingley or Old Trafford would be Egalitarianism Rules, OK?

The golden years either side of 1900 were, of course, the years of Grace. He came onto the scene as a teenager in 1864, utterly transformed the game in the 'seventies and 'eighties, boomed back to irresistible form in 1895, a bearded giant of 47, and partook of Test cricket as late as 1899, when, still an exceptional figure at the crease but a handicap in the field, he 'plotted' his own omission by asking fellow-selector C. B. Fry, as he arrived later than the others for their meeting at the Sports Club, whether he thought Archie MacLaren ought to play in the next Test match. 'Yes, I do,' said Fry. 'That settles it,' chimed WG – the 'it' being his exclusion. He was within a month of his 51st birthday, and could have been said to have had a good run; but his withdrawal left a void not dissimilar in scale to the Avon Gorge. He may not have gone on every tour of Australia (few amateurs found the time), but he *was* cricket. More than that: he was a pillar of English life.

W. G. Grace's influence was to last long after his final appearance in first-class cricket, at The Oval in 1908, and his death in 1915 shook the nation almost as much as Churchill's fifty years later. For decades Dr William Gilbert Grace had been perhaps the most famous man in England, rivalling Gladstone and the Prince of Wales. His beard, his bulk, and his batsmanship ensured this. He took the art to new heights, driving even the most fearsome of bowlers to the boundary and to distraction, reducing them to bowling almost out of the reach of his barndoor bat. He combined forward-play with back-play, struck perilous shooters into the far distances, revealed abnormal reserves of stamina, overawed players and spectators, overwhelmed opponents physically and psychologically, and sometimes overbowled himself. He made 54,896 runs and 126 centuries in first-class cricket, figures that have been overtaken, against expectation, even if his preeminence has not. He remains the most famous cricketer of them all, and he elevated the game in public esteem.

Fry once compared him to Henry the Eighth, who, like WG, was a legend and premier athlete in England long before becoming overweighted with flesh and sundry complications. No-one can calculate the exact depth of WG's influence, though E. B. V. Christian was one of many who attempted to frame The Champion's supremacy in this verse, which he attributed to his cousin:

The bat is, as the sonnet is, but small;
Yet with it batsmen, a stouthearted band,
Waged ceaseless, changing conflict with the ball,
Till Grace arose; and in his mighty hand
The thing became a sceptre, which he wields
Unchallenged yet, Lord of the Playing Fields.

There were others, of course. Most of them were batsmen, for then, as now, bowlers were the drudges. It was an age of so-called classical batsmanship inasmuch as style, fostered at the public schools, was upheld practically as an end in itself. Nor would it have been too difficult to excel at the drive off the front foot when bowling was consistently directed at the off stump and the length was honourably full. Indeed, short balls and legside deliveries almost mandatorily brought forth an apology from the bowler. One evening at Hove, Ranjitsinhji proclaimed the pride of that generation of batsmen when he loudly deplored a mark made on his flimsy leg-guards by the ball, though the pioneers of the pull, the sweep, and the unabashed 'cow shot', such as Walter Read and the two senior Graces, were less fussy, as was Gilbert Jessop, the greatest of improvisators and one of the strongest and most dramatic of hitters, all crouching five-foot-seven of him.

With the coming of swerve bowling and the googly (sneered at by some as nothing more than a gimmick and an unsportsmanlike ploy) the game lost some more of its innocence: the flowing forward-play was stunted, batsmen worked more within their creases, and such magnificent back-foot players as Jack Hobbs of England, Charles Macartney of Australia, and Herby Taylor of South Africa emerged. The princely ranks of MacLaren, Palairet, Jackson, Stoddart, Ranji, Fry, Spooner, Trumper, all picturesque dispatchers of the ball to the sightscreen – where one existed – were absorbed by the years, like a lost legion, with few heirs.

While cricket's evolution did not halt with the Great War, the game in 1914, while different in attitude, was not much removed *technically* from the cricket of today. The six-ball over, a new ball after 200 runs, six runs for hits out of the playing area, the declaration, a wider bowling crease, the follow-on – all these areas of conduct were established. Boards of Control had been set up in England in 1898 and Australia in 1905, and the Imperial (later democratically broadened to International) Cricket

Conference came into being in the summer of 1909. Compared with today's broad conglomerate of full and associate member countries, the original ICC was cosily select, consisting of MCC, Australia, and South Africa. Not even Philadelphia, then a force in the game, was granted admission.

English tours abroad were now firmly under the control of MCC, the sometimes haphazard exploits of privately-promoted Test tours left behind in the nineteenth century. The touring cricketers from England were ambassadors, showing the flag in the colonies, providing a fond link for the settlers from the Old Country and a sight of some curiosity for the native-born. In turn, Australian and South African cricketers were expected to be rough-hewn, and they often were. They were additionally expected to lose, and often did. And sometimes they won, and it did nothing to weaken the bonds of the farflung Empire. Indeed, the ethics of cricket, as exemplified in Newbolt's oft-quoted and oft-parodied *Vitaï Lampada*, were inextricably bound up in the most dramatic of all struggles. With the Gattling jammed and the Colonel dead and the regiment blind with dust and smoke, 'the voice of a schoolboy rallies the ranks: "Play up! play up! and play the game!"' The verse would have been an inspiration on the bumping pitches and in the blinding light of Omdurman and Ladysmith and Mafeking.

It was at Mafeking that the dashing Yorkshire amateur Frank Milligan was mortally wounded during Plumer's attempt to relieve Baden-Powell's garrison. Brought down from his horse by Boer rifle-fire, he had to be left by his fellow skirmishers, who could do nothing to save him. In his personal effects was a Yorkshire fixture-card for the 1900 season. 'He could not guess,' stated the report sorrowfully, 'that he had played his last match.'

Cricketers streamed out to the conflict. Major R. M. Poore, only a few months after scoring 1499 runs at an average of 107 for Hampshire, went to the USA to buy mules for the Government, then set out for the scattered front. Jack Ferris, who with Charlie Turner had formed one of Australia's most successful bowling partnerships ever before joining Gloucestershire, went to war with Colonel Byng's South Australian Light Horse, and died from fever. Prince Christian Victor, a grandson of Queen Victoria, and fine wicketkeeper-batsman at Wellington and Oxford, died in Pretoria from enteric fever a few weeks before Ferris, leaving the monarch sleepless and averse to food in her grief. Not only the young were claimed. George Strachan, the old Surrey and Gloucestershire player, was another fever victim at 51, while in charge of a concentration camp in the Transvaal. As plaintive as any was the fate of Commander Egerton, whose legs were blown off by a shell. 'That ends my cricket!' he is said to have cried. It ended his life.

On the more felicitous side, South African batsman Jimmy Sinclair was so large that the quartermaster of Little's Scouts could not manage to find a patrol jacket to fit him in the whole of Sterkstroom or Naauwpoort.

The struggle went on, but cricket kept its head down. It was to take a global war a dozen or so years later to cause bats and balls to be laid aside, with WG himself, in a letter to the Press, urging all sportsmen to take up arms.

During the last few of Victoria's 63 years on the throne crowds continued to flock not only to the Test matches but to County Championship games, patronising them in numbers such as no modern midweek spectator – *rara avis* that he is – would readily credit. The Oxford–Cambridge annual match, too, drew big attendances, as did the Gentlemen–Players. Even the Eton *v* Harrow at Lord's, then still a vogue occasion, was viewed by deep ranks of gentlemen in grey toppers and morning coats, with their elegant, corseted ladies, ankles covered, parasols on high.

From international to school match, there was but one way to see them on the move – and the same applied to the rarely-seen Queen – and that was *in the flesh*. The conveniently communicative yet dehumanising electronic age was some way off, even if Marconi in 1901 was picking up the first Transatlantic wireless signal, transmitted from Cornwall to Newfoundland, and even if Lumière and Paul were busy with their brief and jerky moving pictures.

How were the hypnotic and beneficent effects of cricket evaluated during those years of hansom cabs and gaslight, of negligible income tax and flimsy wages, when no women and only 58 per cent of men in Britain had a vote? J. M. Barrie, creator of Peter Pan, speaking at an Authors' Club dinner in honour of P. F. Warner,* England's triumphant captain in Australia in 1903–04, said he had read the news of

the victory while walking along Piccadilly 'with hansoms and four-wheelers passing over me constantly'. But he scarcely felt them!

Barrie said he thought that the man who invented cricket 'did a bigger thing than the man who wrote *Hamlet*'. The same William Shakespeare was utilised by *Punch* after Warwickshire's memorable first Championship in 1911. In F. H. Townsend's cartoon, the Immortal Bard says to the successful young captain, Frank Foster: 'Warwick, thou art worthy!' (*Henry VI*). It was a popular win, for until Kent's first Championship in 1906 no county outside the Big Six – Surrey, Nottinghamshire, Middlesex, Yorkshire, Gloucestershire, and Lancashire – had won the title in 42 years of reckoning. Today almost any of the seventeen counties has fair prospects of taking the title.

A clue to the attraction of cricket came during the tour of Australia by Stoddart's team in 1894–95, when the five Test matches generated an excitement seldom equalled before or since. It was even reputed that the little silver-haired Queen herself, not renowned as a cricket enthusiast, eagerly perused the cabled reports dispatched from the distant colony by the pioneering *Pall Mall Gazette*. Three years later, when Australia thrashed the visiting Englishmen four Tests to one, it was seriously suggested that Harry Trott and his team

*A third choice as captain, incidentally. The series was won without the services of F. S. Jackson and C. B. Fry, who were forced to decline the leadership. A. C. MacLaren had already declined Australia's invitation to take out another team.

of Victorians, South Australians, and New South Welshmen had done more for the movement towards the country's Federation than all the posturing, agitating politicians put together.

Conan Doyle doted on the game, and was a useful player; perhaps as many as 300 of his characters had names suggested by those of cricketers with whom he was familiar. The creator of Sherlock Holmes took only one wicket in first-class cricket; but it was worth at least a dozen others: it was W. G. Grace's, and Doyle wrote a 19-stanza 'epic' verse to commemorate his triumph. Then there was his brother-in-law, E. W. Hornung, who launched the cricketing burglar Raffles upon an unsuspecting public. Even he, though, fell sad in 1915:

No Lord's this year; no silken lawn on which
A dignified and dainty throng meanders.
The Schools take guard upon a fiercer pitch
Somewhere in Flanders.

Siegfried Sassoon, Ernest Raymond, A. A. Milne, E. V. Lucas – they and many others in the literary field nurtured longings for the sunlit field that expressed themselves in their work. And then there was Wodehouse. PGW had opened the bowling for Dulwich College at the turn of the century with Neville Knox, who was to return some devastating performances for Surrey and the Gentlemen before his shins gave way. Until disenchantment set in years later, Wodehouse derived much joy – and considerable revenue – from engaging 'Mike Jackson' in a stream of cricketing escapades. It is quite well-known, too, that Jeeves, one of the two most

famous butlers of all time, was named after a Warwickshire all-rounder, who perished in the Great War.

Nostalgia comes and goes. The most celebrated of laments known to cricket was written by the wretched Lancastrian Francis Thompson, some years after Wilfrid Meynell had retrieved him from his pestilent drug-ridden twilight world on the Thames Embankment. Sitting at Lord's, he thinks of the Red Rose team of 1878:

I look through my tears on a soundless-clapping host
As the run-stealers flicker to and fro,
To and fro:—
O my Hornby and my Barlow long ago!

Hornby was a dasher, on the rugby as well as the cricket field; but it was a source of wonder that anybody should have pined for Dick Barlow, who specialised in such monstrosities as five runs in two-and-a-half hours (twice in county matches) and 90 in almost six hours (in a Test against Australia, evoking some satirical verse in *Punch*). Yet upon reflection, this is probably exactly the kind of patience tied to pain that appealed to Thompson's tortured mind.

Rather surprisingly, we find E. V. Lucas sufficiently disgruntled in 1906 to write that 'not only has cricket lost many of its old simplicities, it has lost its characters too. In the late process of levelling up, or levelling down, individuality has suffered.' That has a modern ring about it. So does a paragraph in the *Daily Graphic* in July, 1907: 'The medical profession tell us that nervous symptoms are strongly marked in the diseases of the present day, and that deaths from nervous breakdown are rapidly increasing. Perhaps the reason for this may be found in the nervous tension of this age. Weaklings resort to strong drugs to fight off debility and disease, and deceive themselves with so-called nerve tonics and cure-alls.' In *Wisden* the mighty Surrey and England fast bowler Tom Richardson, emphatically never a weakling, was endorsing the virtues of Dr Williams' Pink Pills, which had relieved his rheumatic joints: 'When I retired from county cricket,' testified the Titan turned publican, 'my nervous system was impaired. I began to get upset over trivial matters. My appetite fell off, and my memory often failed me. But the most worrying trouble was insomnia.'

Civilisation, or more precisely industrialisation, was advancing too rapidly even then. The motor car was driving the horse off the highway at such a rate that machines simulating the trot, canter and gallop were marketed to stimulate the liver and quicken the circulation.

Andrew Lang's *Ballade of Dead Cricketers*, an elegy to the great players of Hambledon, can have done little to swell ground attendances in his own time. It needed someone to put a perspective upon it, as it always does, and C. B. Fry, in earnest vein, wrote, in his 1939 autobiography: 'I have a notion that the cricket of the 'nineties and early nineteen-hundreds was more amusing to watch, but I am not at all sure that the game of today is not more difficult to play. The fast bowling, however, were it here, would make a difference.' E. E. Bowen, of Harrow fame, summed it up in lighter lines:

There were wonderful giants of old, you know,
There were wonderful giants of old;
They grew more mightily, all of a row,
Than ever was heard or told;
All of them stood their six-feet-four,
And they threw to a hundred yards or more,
And never were lame or stiff or sore;
And we, compared to the days of yore,
Are cast in a pigmy mould.

Beyond argument there was an abundance of cricket glory in those years, but, viewed from the 1970s, it was less a remote and isolated period than a halfway house. A match to assert this was that between England and Australia at Trent Bridge in May, 1905. In England's large second innings Warwick Armstrong resorted to negative bowling wide of leg stump to a packed legside field during the Jackson-Rhodes partnership, tactics that wrongly have come to be regarded as peculiarly modern, and which brought heaps of criticism down upon Armstrong, though it was not missed by all observers that the batsmen ignored the bait despite England's position of strength. Then, on the third and last afternoon, Australia were struggling to avoid defeat. Victor Trumper's back injury prevented him from batting, and as wickets continued to fall, a remarkable incident occurred, something which positively could not have been seen as typical in the fanatical competitiveness of sport in the 1970s. Australian batsman Charlie McLeod ran to the pavilion to ask his captain if he should appeal against the light, which was growing poorer by the minute. The umpires would almost certainly have agreed to suspend play, but Joe Darling ruled out any appeal. Australia had been outplayed, and harboured no desire to escape in this way. In considering the captain's sense of chivalry, that of McLeod, who need not have consulted him, deserves approval.

County cricket's following was ardent, at a peak. Surrey were the only county to match Yorkshire, and won the Championship in 1887, 1888, 1889 (shared), 1890, 1891, 1892, 1894, 1895, 1899, and 1914, never to win it again until the 1950s, when they made up for lost time. Grubby Kennington Oval echoed to Cockney cheers through the years of 'Obbs, 'Ayward, 'Ayes, 'Olland, 'Enderson, 'Itch, not forgetting 'Habel'. The amateurs came and went, but the feeling was pronounced: this was the working-men's ground of the South – with Leyton catering for the East Enders.

They might have been Ovalites or Essex-followers whose exchange was quoted in a 1900 edition of *Cricket*: Scene – top of a bus, Sunday morning. Gentleman in shirtsleeves, looking at newspaper: 'This yer Fry and old Bosun-quett 'ave been and done it *this* time, any way.' Gentleman in very cheap flannel suit: 'What might they 'ave done?' 'Why the've both bin and made an 'undred in each innings.' 'Well, I don't see nothing in that. Old WG, he done it three times, and so did young Fawrster.' 'I didn't say as they 'adn't, but they never done it both at the same time, did they?' 'No, can't say as they did. It *do* make a difference, of course.'

The notable pride verging on insularity associated with Kent was even then strengthening, aided by the county's first-ever Championship in 1906, which was hotly pursued by others in 1909,

1910, and 1913. *Cricket* in December 1912 was critical: 'I do think sometimes that the Kent cricket crowd is just a little *too* much wrapped up in Kent's doings. "Seen an evening paper?" I asked a Kentish partisan at the end of one of those grey days. "Yes. Nothing done at Dover," he answered. "What of the Test match?" "Oh, Frank Woolley's going strong – 5 for 29." What was the Australian total? That he did not know! What had happened on other grounds? He really hadn't noticed! And he was not the only one of his kind whom I met.'

Not that they were much less committed up North, where factory chimneys coincidentally but invariably belched extra smoke when the visiting batsmen were trying to get a sight of the ball. At Bramall Lane, Sheffield, where the grinders constituted as tough and demanding an audience as any, a fieldsman risked smutty trousers if he reclined on the turf during a break in play.

Country-house cricket was enjoying its heyday, played by carefully-chosen teams on the private grounds of some of the more sporting landlords of England, mostly in the South. There the gentlemen of such clubs as I Zingari, Free Foresters, the Grasshoppers, and Eton Ramblers played their cricket, exercised impeccable table manners (if they desired a return invitation), and danced the evening away. Through a colourful splash of blazers and hat-ribbons, the umpires – butlers, gamekeepers or gardeners of His Lordship – would commence proceedings, which comprised an exhibition of all that was attractive and honourable in the summer pastime. Country-house cricket as it was then staged became next to extinct after the Great War, a poignant loss for those survivors who had been part of it.

Club cricket had gone its informal way for many seasons, and it took the War to bring about some organised administration in the South. The Club Cricket Conference was founded in 1915 in an endeavour to keep clubs together. The headlong rush into competitive league cricket on Saturdays which came just over half a century later would have horrified the majority of club cricketers of Victoria's and Edward's time.

Not that club cricket was 'soft'. County amateurs played regularly with local clubs, and usually put personal performance before patronising gesture. Precedents had been set in the 1880s with quadruple-centuries by J. S. Carrick and A. E. Stoddart – both at least partly immune from criticism by the absence of a law permitting declarations – and with the second-wicket stand of 605 by A. H. Trevor and G. F. Vernon in the Orleans Club's innings of 920 at Rickling Green. There was no lack of sincerity about these feats.

A conversation overheard in the spring of 1900* further dispels suggestions that club cricket, if loosely organised, was soft: Scene – An office in the City, Monday morning. 'Hallo Jack, what's up?' 'Beastly stiff. Played in a match on Saturday.' 'How did you bowl?' 'I began with three wides, and the batsman said that it was dashed rot to send such a fool against a good team. The next ball hit him hard on the funny bone and nearly made him howl; as it

went on and took his wicket he was pretty sick. Then I hit another man on the chin and bowled *him*, and he said it was a beastly shame to try a fast bowler on such a wicket.' 'Did you go off?' 'Yes, about twenty minutes afterwards. But they were all out then!'

Enthusiasm was never enough, however, and when Dr L. O. S. Poidevin, an Australian who played cricket for Lancashire and Davis Cup tennis for Australasia, expressed the belief in 1910 that 'club cricket in this country is too magnificently disorganised to ever do itself justice or reach anything above hopeless mediocrity in standard of play' he was pinpointing a shortcoming that to this day has had some bearing upon England's fortunes in international cricket. Club cricket in Australia and South Africa was already well established as a supply-line to the first-class ranks.

Where disciplines *were* introduced at the sub-senior levels in England by the Victorians was in the leagues of the North and Midlands. In 1888 the Birmingham League was formed, in 1890 the Lancashire League, and by the end of the century countless clubs in Yorkshire, Durham, Northumberland, Cheshire, and Staffordshire had title honours to play – and play hard – for, with mayors of boroughs accepting club presidencies and more benevolent millowners taking an active interest. It was almost entirely amateur – the time of famous professionals on lucrative contracts lay in the years after 1918 – but it was keen. . . .

Just as, in its own way, village cricket was keen. The vicars and 'squires' and

*From *Cricket: A Weekly Record of the Game.*

blacksmiths of today somehow have a less authentic aura about them than the characters who lunge, trip and laugh their way through the pages of Sassoon, Macdonell, and de Selincourt. Then, as now, the oddly-attired men and youths who cavorted on rude fields in approximate accordance with the Laws of Cricket were considered the very soul of the game, though an England Test XI has hardly ever contained a player with such rustic beginnings. That, many a villager would claim defiantly, is something of which to be proud.

Village cricketers, metropolitan club cricketers, county cricketers, cricketers from all corners of the Empire: they fell by the hundred and thousand in the filthy mud at Ypres, at Loos, at Arras, at the Somme, at Neuve Chapelle, at Mons, at Gallipoli. The 1915 *Wisden Cricketers' Almanack* listed 44 war casualties, the 1916 edition 285, 1917 almost 500 (plus a reprieve for Cambridge and Gloucestershire cricketer Rev. A. H. C. Fargus, who, it was discovered, had missed his train, leaving the *Monmouth* to sail to its Pacific doom without him). The 1918 *Wisden* told of over 400 war deaths, plus 84 from previous years, and the 1919 Almanack listed 330, with another 46 lately advised from 1917, including Australian fast bowler Albert 'Tibby' Cotter, aged 33, who enlisted with the Australian Light Horse and was slain at Beersheba when he raised his classical brow above the trench, doubting the scene reflected in his army issue periscope. Another casualty of some sporting significance was Norman Callaway, whose solitary innings for New South Wales, in February 1915, amounted to 207 runs in as many minutes. What cricket-field glories might have awaited a batsman of such demonstrable potential?

Most of the slaughtered were young and had played for this or that public school, and sometimes for a University and county. Clifton College alone lost more than 500 of her sons in the conflict, one of whom was 23-year-old Lieut. G. W. E. Whitehead, of the Royal Flying Corps, attached to the Royal Air Force. He was killed less than a month before the war ended. Captain of the College eleven in 1913 and 1914, he had already made a score of 259 not out against Liverpool, and if any individual tribute could be said to speak for the tragic depletion of British manhood, 'An Old Cliftonian's' might:

George Whitehead was a perfect flower of the public schools. He was not limited to athletics only, great though he was in this respect. Intellectually he was far above the average, and was as happy with a good book as when he was scoring centuries. His ideals were singularly high and though gentle and broad-minded, he always stood uncompromisingly for all that was clean. So modest was he, that strangers sometimes failed to realise his worth.

Well might J. C. Squire, another of the cricket-loving poets of the time, have written: 'My God,' said God, 'I've got my work cut out.'

DAVID FRITH   Guildford 1978

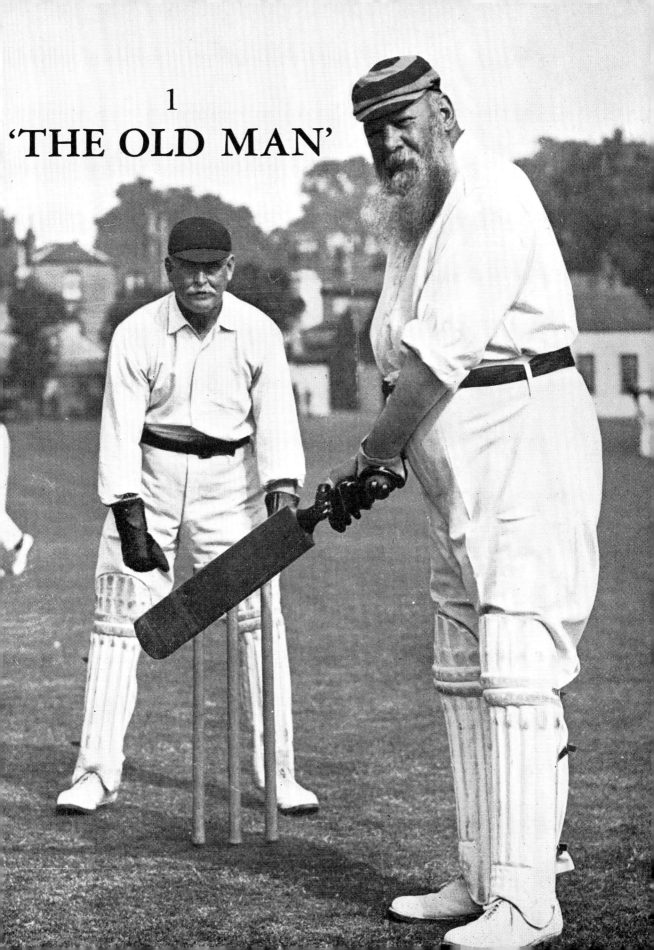

1

'THE OLD MAN'

Dr W. G. Grace, by now a familiar figure on the cricket grounds of England for more than thirty years, pictured during one of his last games for Gloucestershire, probably at Cheltenham. Perhaps he is checking on his batting order. Certainly he had little need of the tobacco kiosk. The picture is taken from a magic lantern slide by local schoolmaster Alfred George, whose closeness to the great cricketer has not affected the steadiness of his camera-grip

Right: Buckling on his pads for a new innings, as he did almost 1500 times in major matches and a great many times in lesser games

Below: WG, the whale no net could capture, though the photographer in the panama hat attempts to do so on film. In spite of his bulk, The Champion's left elbow assumes a high position of command

Above: After his break with Gloucestershire, WG, living in south-east London, managed the London County team, whose home ground was a dangerous stone's throw from the celebrated Crystal Palace. Here many lesser-known cricketers had a chance to play with and against the great man. *Left:* The John Bull presence of W. G. Grace oozes from this snapshot taken by one of his 'occasional' players, G. H. V. Hooper. It remained unpublished for seventy years

W. G. Grace plays for – and leads – England for the last time, Trent Bridge, June 1899. It is also Wilfred Rhodes's first Test appearance. Back row: R. G. Barlow (umpire), T. W. Hayward, G. H. Hirst, W. Gunn, J. T. Hearne (twelfth man), W. Storer, W. Brockwell, V. A. Titchmarsh (umpire); seated: C. B. Fry, K. S. Ranjitsinhji, W. G. Grace, F. S. Jackson; front: W. Rhodes, J. T. Tyldesley

WG came of solid Gloucestershire stock. Here, stretching the age limits either way, a Grace family eleven is mustered in 1891. Back row: Edward, Henry, Gerald, Arthur, George; front: WG junior, WG, Alfred, Francis, Edward Mills Grace (an eminent elder brother), and Alfie. A brother, Fred, had died in 1880, aged only 29, a fortnight after playing alongside WG and EM in the Oval Test match against Australia. WG's son, pictured beside him here, also died young – aged 30, in 1905, after an operation for appendicitis

Few men can remain stiff-lipped with a baby beckoning for attention, least of all if it is one's own grandson. WG is thinner on top than his small descendant, though the child has a long way to go to challenge the facial growth

Among the other sides of WG (he was, after all, a qualified medical practitioner, a keen golfer and beagler, and a superb athlete in his youth) was a weakness for lawn bowls. He was the first president of the English Bowls Association, and is here signalling a 'toucher'

Left: Almost everything about him would invite comment – mostly derogatory – today. The girth, the dark shoes, the grubby pads, the well-worn bat – but the threat to the bowled ball is real, and after the drive through cover has done its work the bowler, like so many of his breed, is left to contemplate the hopelessness of it all. *Right:* Another century for WG – this time 175 not out for London County against Worcestershire on the beautiful ground by the River Severn, in 1899

WG with his Gloucestershire team, the setting which will always seem the most appropriate for the doctor from Downend. In this 1894 group are: back row – H. Wrathall, J. Painter, Smith (scorer), W. Murch, F. G. Roberts; seated – Dr E. M. Grace, Capt. A. T. H. Newnham, Dr W. G. Grace, J. J. Ferris, S. A. P. Kitcat; front – W. Troup, J. H. Board, H. W. Brown. It was a difficult year for the county: they lost 13 out of 16 matches, and WG averaged only 18.29. At 46, they said, what could be expected of him, no matter what his amazing past achievements? Then, in 1895, he came back with a spectacular display – his hundredth hundred (a score of 288) at Taunton, 257 at Gravesend, 169 at Lord's to take him past a thousand runs in the month of May. His return for the season was 2346 runs at an average of 51, and it really began to seem that he was indestructible

On July 16, 17 and 18, 1906 (the last date being W. G. Grace's 58th birthday) the Grand Old Man captained the Gentlemen against the Players at The Oval. His second innings – his 151st for the Gentlemen since his debut in 1865 – brought him 74 birthday runs, the highest of the match for the amateurs. He was seen to be, not unnaturally, 'feeling the exertion' after reaching fifty in an hour and three-quarters. Accompanying WG as the Gentlemen take the field is fellow Gloucestershire cricketer G. L. Jessop. *Below:* WG, now white-bearded, with the Eltham team in July 1914, fifteen months before his death. His last cricket match was for Eltham against Grove Park on July 25, 1914, and he scored 69 not out. His son, CB is standing third from the right

W. G. Grace (1848–1915), cricket's patriarchal figure, founder of modern batsmanship, almost as highly revered today as when he dominantly bestrode the nineteenth-century cricket fields of England

Drawing by A. Chevallier Tayler

WILL'S
Cigarettes.

MR. C. J. KORTWRIGHT,
ESSEX

1

WILLS'S CIGARETTES.

MR. C. J. B. WOOD (LEICESTER).

2

WILLS'S CIGARETTES.

MR. G. L. JESSOP (GLO'STER.).

3

WILLS'S
Cigarettes.

MR. G. MACREGOR,
MIDDLESEX.

4

WILLS'S
Cigarettes.

MAJOR POORE,
HAMPSHIRE.

5

WILLS'S
Cigarettes.

MR. C. J. BURNUP,
KENT.

6

"CAPSTAN"
CIGARETTES.

R. A. YOUNG (SUSSEX).

7

WILLS'S
Cigarettes.

A. MOLD,
LANCASHIRE

8

WILLS'S
Cigarettes.

MR. C. E. DE TRAFFORD,
LEICESTERSHIRE.

9

WILLS'S
Cigarettes.

A. WARD,
LANCASHIRE.

10

WILLS'S
Cigarettes.

J. T. HEARNE,
MIDDLESEX.

11

WILLS'S
Cigarettes.

MR. S. M. J. WOODS,
SOMMERSETSHIRE.

12

PERSONALITIES OF THE GOLDEN AGE

1. **Charles Kortright**, a candidate for the title of Fastest Bowler Ever. He never played for England, but in club cricket, for Essex, and for the Gentlemen he was often a figure of terror, capable of bowling a venomous lifting ball on even the slowest wicket and a blinding yorker to defeat even the best batsmen when set

2. **C. J. B. Wood**, a coal merchant, who played as an amateur for Leicestershire between 1896 and 1923, serving as captain in 1914 and immediately after the war. An opening batsman, 'Cis' Wood carried his bat through the innings 17 times, twice (uniquely) in the game against Yorkshire at Bradford in 1911, when he scored 107 not out and 117 not out

3. **Gilbert Jessop**, who, with his unequalled ferocity of strokeplay, practically gave his name to the English language. From 1894 to the Great War he played for Gloucestershire, bowling fast earlier in his career, and always posing a threat to batsmen as a brilliant cover fieldsman. He made 53 centuries, 15 of them inside an hour, and his famous 75-minute hundred at The Oval in 1902 remains the fastest in England-Australia Tests. Small but very strong, 'The Croucher' was called 'The Human Catapult' by startled spectators in the USA

4. **Gregor MacGregor**, Edinburgh-born wicket-keeper for Cambridge University, Middlesex, the Gentlemen, and England, and a Scotland rugby representative. His 'keeping to Sammy Woods's fast bowling for Cambridge – standing up at the stumps – was awesomely skilful and brave

5. **Major R. M. Poore**, whose diligent study of textbooks on batting led to his emergence, if only briefly, into the highest ranks. Playing,

without distinction, for South Africa when England toured in 1895–96, he hit the headlines in 1899 with 1551 runs at 91.23, with seven centuries, the highest 304 against Somerset. Very tall and powerful, he excelled at polo, fencing, shooting, and lawn tennis

6. **Cuthbert 'Pinky' Burnup**, educated at Malvern and Cambridge, and amateur batsman for Kent from 1896 to 1907. He made a century on his first appearance for the Gentlemen against the Players, and surprised many by taking eight wickets in the county's defeat of the 1899 Australian touring team

7. **Richard Young**, one of the few bespectacled cricketers to play for England. He kept wicket and opened the batting, none too successfully, in two of the 1907–08 Tests in Australia while enjoying a very profitable four seasons in the Cambridge XI. He also earned an amateur football cap as an outside-right

8. **Arthur Mold**, Lancashire and England's controversial fast bowler, who, after a dozen highly successful years, was no-balled for throwing, and instantly felt that all his achievements had been discredited. Using only a short run-up, he had a hefty body-swing and could bowl an almost impossibly awkward off-cutter

9. **The Hon. Charles Edmund de Trafford**, whose family seat embraced the Old Trafford Test match ground, captained Leicestershire from 1890 to 1907, and was among the biggest hitters of the day, often disdaining to wear batting gloves, and usually falling to catches in the long-field. His bearing in the field was military and his value to his less than fashionable county team enormous

continued next page

10. Albert Ward, born in Yorkshire, served Lancashire nobly for 14 seasons as a professional batsman, making almost 15,000 runs. His benefit in 1902 yielded over £1700. Among his finest innings were 55, 75, 117, and 93 in his eight Tests against Australia – all now largely forgotten efforts

11. J. T. Hearne, member of a great cricket family, took over 3000 wickets in a splendid career stretching from 1890 to 1914. Moving the ball either way, with great accuracy, he could be unplayable on a bowler's wicket, and against the Australians in 1896 he took 4 for 4 and 9 for 73 for MCC at Lord's. Three years later, in a Test at Leeds, he accomplished probably the finest hat-trick ever in dismissing Hill, Gregory, and Noble. A model professional, in 1920 he was awarded the rare distinction of election to the Middlesex committee

12. Sammy Woods, the popular 'SMJ', born and reared in Australia, became synonymous with Somerset, for whom he played from 1886 to 1907, leading the side wholeheartedly and later serving as club secretary. A rumbustious fast bowler and aggressive batsman, he appeared for Australia at cricket and England at cricket and rugby. He once hit 215 against Sussex, at Hove, in only 2½ hours

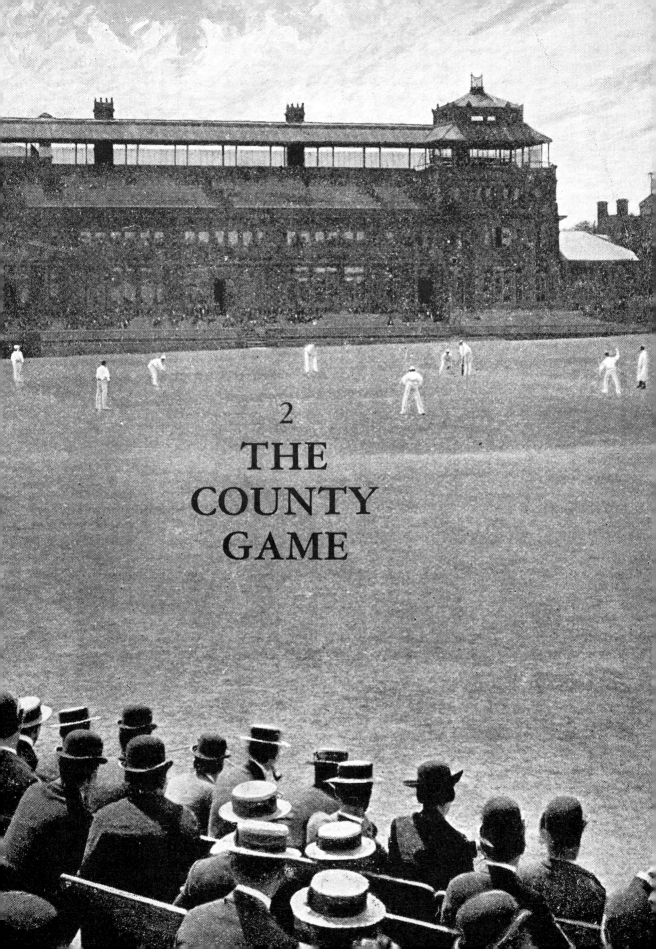

2
THE
COUNTY
GAME

The Taunton ground during Somerset's match against Lancashire in July, 1895. The visitors made 801, Archie MacLaren scoring 424, and won by an innings and 452 runs. The impact of MacLaren's innings, which lasted almost eight hours, was enormous. The public had not become accustomed to huge individual scores, as they were to become during the twentieth century, when Ponsford, Bradman, Hammond and others reached the heady heights of 300, even 400, with some regularity. MacLaren, aged only 23, scored one six, 62 fours, 11 threes, 37 twos, and 63 singles, and added 141 for the first wicket with Albert Ward (64) and 363 for the second with A. G. Paul (177), and the first-class record he beat was W. G. Grace's 344, made in 1876

A warm-up before play by W. H. Patterson, a 'natural' whose career as a solicitor allowed him little cricket until the second half of the summer. All elegance, from his necktie to his smart footwork, he went from Harrow to Oxford, and played for Kent for twenty years to 1900, excelling on wet wickets and surprising constantly with his ability to do well without practice. *Below:* Bobby Abel tips his cap as the members at The Oval show their pleasure at his 357 not out against Somerset in May, 1899. He put on 334 with Hayward for the fourth wicket and 212 with V. F. S. ('Very Fast Scoring') Crawford for the sixth. Many a worthy innings has been played at The Oval since, but the well-known gas-holders have peeped down upon only one higher: Len Hutton's 364 for England in 1938

The hallowed Long Room in the pavilion at Lord's has its spring cleaning at the turn of the century. Many of the paintings are still on exhibition, though MCC's collection of art and relics has swelled over the years to such an extent that much of it has to be preserved out of sight. What oceans of comment have risen in this sacred hall since it was erected in 1890

Yorkshire won nine County Championships between 1893 and 1912, establishing a narrow lead over Surrey by the First World War that has since been extended massively. The 1894 team pictured are: back row – H. Turner (scorer), T. Wardall, L. Whitehead, M. J. Dodsworth (vice-president), J. Mounsey, H. Draper (umpire); seated – J. Tunnicliffe, R. Peel, Lord Hawke (captain), Hon. F. S. Jackson, E. Wainwright; front – J. T. Brown, D. Hunter, G. H. Hirst. Nine of the eleven players are professionals

Worcester's wickets have invariably been excellent, and the tradition goes back to the days of Fred Hunt (with dog) and his ground staff, pictured in 1899, when Worcestershire at last became a first-class county after having won the Minor Counties competition in the three previous years. The New Road ground had an agricultural air about it for some years: once 210 sheep, seven horses, three cows, and heaps of manure had to be cleared before a county match could start. *Below:* Warwickshire's ground at Edgbaston in the 1890s, showing the original pavilion, which has been embraced by new structure in a startling building development which took place after the Second World War. It was here in 1902 that Australia were bowled out for 36 in a Test match

J.R. MASON CATCHES THE LANCASHIRE CAPTAIN VIA HUISH

F.H. HUISH
E. HUMPHREYS
C. BLYTHE
A. FIELDER

LORD HARRIS DISTRIBUTES THE MONEY COLLECTED ON TUESDAY AND THURSDAY FOR THE KENTISH PROFESSIONALS

ARTHUR FIELDER. MAINLY RESPONSIBLE FOR THE DOWNFALL OF LANCASHIRE.

Kent steam towards their first-ever County Championship. In August, 1906 they beat a strong Lancashire side at Canterbury by an innings. Hutchings made 176, Burnup 94, Mason 88, and Fielder took eleven wickets, Blythe eight. For the visitors Spooner 'bagged a pair' and MacLaren sent an old gentleman to hospital after cracking him on the forehead with a lofted drive. The *Daily Graphic* sketch shows his second-innings downfall. It also gives an impression of Lord Harris handing out the professionals' bonuses

Canon F. H. Gillingham plays a ball from Rhodes in the Essex v Yorkshire match in May 1908 at Leyton, where Gillingham was a curate. Born in Tokyo in 1875, he came to Essex via Dulwich College and Durham University, and the feature of his play was robust driving. He played for the county for a quarter of a century from 1903, with this season of 1908 his best. He scored 79 in this innings. His partner is J. W. H. T. Douglas, with Hunter keeping wicket. Gillingham was at the microphone when the first cricket radio commentary was made in 1927, and in 1939 he was appointed chaplain to King George VI. *Right:* Wilfred Rhodes goes out to bat in his benefit match, the 'Roses match' at Bramall Lane, Sheffield. He was given only a third of the total takings of £750, the rest being invested for him, and Yorkshire felt obliged to launch a separate appeal fund, which raised the final sum to £2200. The dour and canny cricketer bought a cottage in Marsh, near Huddersfield, and lived there with his wife for over forty years

The voice of Lord's, F. E. (later Sir Francis) Lacey, who was MCC secretary from 1898 (when he succeeded the red-bearded Henry Perkins) until 1926. A barrister, Lacey was a very successful young batsman at Sherborne School and for Dorset before playing for Hampshire for almost twenty years up to 1897. In 1887, eight years before Hampshire gained first-class status, he made a record 323 not out at Southampton against Norfolk. Under his firm administration the Marylebone Club prospered and its control of domestic and certain overseas matters tightened. *Below:* An impression in oils by A. Chevallier Tayler of the Kent v Lancashire contest at Canterbury in 1906 (see page 41). Blythe bowls to Tyldesley, whose scores of 19 and 4 paled beside his 295 not out against the same opponents two months earlier on his home ground of Old Trafford

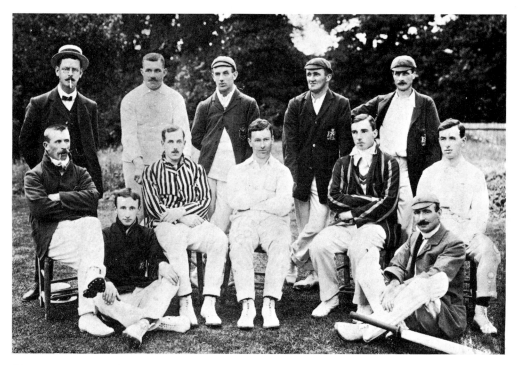

Glamorgan, the only 'foreign' side in the English County Championship, were not granted first-class status until 1921. Before that they were not without considerable talent, much of which resided in this 1908 group: back row – J. Davies (scorer), Sgt Thomas, P. Morris, Preedy, A. Nash; seated – W. J. Bancroft, N. V. H. Riches, A. Gibson (captain), T. A. L. Whittington, H. Thomas; front – J. G. Symonds, H. Creber. Bancroft, one of the greatest of Welsh rugby footballers, was engaged as a professional in 1895 at £2 a week. *Below:* The Surrey professionals take the field under an overcast sky at The Oval. The paid men lived separate lives to those of their amateur brethren

Top: Surrey fast bowler Bill Hitch hurls one down to Kent's wicketkeeper Fred Huish – whose backlift leaves nothing to be desired – in the Championship match at The Oval in August, 1909. Strudwick keeps wicket. *The lower picture* shows J. R. Mason reaching his century later in the innings – his third in succession. He and Blythe added 141 in 70 minutes for the tenth wicket, and Kent won by nine wickets

P. A. 'Peter' Perrin, a batting stalwart for Essex from 1896 to 1928, comes in after making an unbeaten 343 against Derbyshire at Chesterfield in 1904: 272 came in boundaries, the field being on the small side. The other ingredients, according to *Cricket* magazine, were 'a fine wicket, an extremely hot day, weak bowling, and brilliant batting'. He was 295 not out at the end of the opening day. Surprisingly, Essex went on to lose by nine wickets. Their 597 was matched by 548, the black Jamaican Charles Ollivierre scoring 229, and they collapsed for 97 to the bowling of Warren and Bestwick in the second innings. Ollivierre steered Derbyshire to an extraordinary victory with 92 not out

Cricket has always had a vast unseen audience. In the Golden Age it depended on newspaper coverage and word of mouth. News placards were often fervent – but alarmist to the uninitiated. In this 1896 *Punch* cartoon the gentleman gasps 'Collapse of Essex! Dear, dear! I wonder if my property at Ilford is safe?'

Warwickshire surprised the cricket world by winning the County Championship in 1911, under their young captain Frank Foster. The Midland heroes pictured are: back row – W. C. Hands, E. J. Smith, Rev. J. H. Parsons, C. Charlesworth, S. Kinneir; seated – S. Santall, F. G. Stephens, F. R. Foster (captain), G. W. Stephens, E. F. Field; front – William Quaife, C. S. Baker. They were a remarkably long-lived bunch of men: Kinneir died youngest, at 57, and Charlesworth reached 78, Quaife 79, F. G. Stephens (a twin) 81, Santall 83, Hands 87, Baker 93, and at the time of writing Jack Parsons is 87 and 'Tiger' Smith, the world's oldest Test survivor, is 92. *Below:* The attractive ground at Bath early in the century. As is commonly seen, two ladies have better things to do than watch cricket

The Southampton ground has changed little over the years, though the semi-formal dress, the tents, and the absence of raucousness give the old-time scene a pleasant dignity and tranquillity missing from the rowdy exercises in partisanship which are often the product of modern limited-overs matches

Tom Hayward (1871–1939), one of England's and Surrey's two great Cambridge-born runmakers – the other his opening partner Hobbs. Hayward passed a thousand runs every season from 1895 to 1914, reaching a then-record 3518 in 1906. The following year he made four centuries in two matches in six days. He was the second batsman, following Grace, to score a century of centuries, and forty times he and Hobbs posted a hundred for the first wicket. A master of the off-drive and the cut, Hayward's top score was 315 not out against Lancashire in 1898, at The Oval (where he made 58 of his centuries). Upon hearing that a cash award had been made to Jack Brown for a triple-century scored the same week for Yorkshire at Chesterfield, Hayward, a professional through and through, declared that he would make do with single centuries in future. Happily for the crowds he broke that vow half-a-dozen times

Vanity Fair drawing by 'Spy

BRAUND

1

F. A. TARRANT (MIDDLESEX).

2

MR. C. H. B. MARSHAM (KENT).

3

MR. J. N. CRAWFORD (SURREY).

4

WILL'S'S Cigarettes.

A. TROTT. MIDDLESEX.

5

WILL'S'S Cigarettes.

G. H. HIRST, YORKSHIRE.

6

KNIGHT

7

R. S. LUCAS. MIDDLESEX

8

ARNOLD

9

MR. PERCY A. PERRIN (ESSEX).

10

A. R. WARREN (DERBYSHIRE),

11

FIELDER

12

PERSONALITIES OF THE GOLDEN AGE

1. Len Braund, a magnificent all-rounder whom Surrey let go early in his career. He served Somerset and England as batsman (three Test hundreds), leg-spin bowler, and glorious slip fielder, achieving the 'double' in 1901, 1902, and 1903, later coaching Cambridge and becoming a first-class umpire. Both his legs were amputated during the years of the Second World War

2. Frank Tarrant, an Australian, who passed 1000 runs and 100 wickets in each of the eight seasons preceding the Great War. A sound batsman, his highest score for Middlesex was 250 not out, and five times he took nine wickets in an innings with his slow-medium left-arm bowling. Had he stayed in Australia he would certainly have played Test cricket. After the war he became a successful racehorse-dealer in India and his home country

3. C. H. B. Marsham, of Eton, Oxford, and Kent, led the county to their first Championship in 1906. Like a number of other amateurs, he was never in the top class as a cricketer, but his influence and leadership were to the pronounced benefit of the game, which his family served for a century and a half. Cloudesley Marsham saw action with the West Kent Yeomanry in Egypt, Gallipoli, and Palestine

4. Jack Crawford, a schoolboy prodigy at Repton, played for Surrey and England while in his teens, and took 30 wickets in the 1907–08 series in Australia. Bespectacled, he hit with astonishing power, and bowled fast-medium. In 1909 he went to Australia after a dispute with his county, and during a tour of New Zealand he scored 354 against a local side at Temuka, adding 298 with Victor Trumper in 69 minutes, hitting 14 sixes and 45 fours

5. Albert Trott, who took 8 for 43 on his debut for Australia against England in 1894–95 and averaged 102.50 for the series, was later ignored by the selectors, and so started a career as a professional for Middlesex. A gargantuan hitter, he drove M. A. Noble over the Lord's pavilion, via a chimney pot, in 1899, and as a bowler of mainly fast but varying deliveries he often proved irresistible, nine times taking eight wickets in an innings and once all ten. He shortened his own benefit match by taking four wickets in four balls and then a hat-trick, against Somerset in 1907, and in 1899 and 1900 he recorded over 1000 runs and 200 wickets. His powers waned after 1904, and he became an umpire after his retirement in 1910. He shot himself on the eve of the Great War

6. George Hirst, the perfection of an all-round professional cricketer. Short but broadly-built, he established a unique record in 1906 with over 2000 runs and 200 wickets, and served Yorkshire regularly from 1892 until 1921 as right-hand batsman and left-arm swerve bowler. He made over 36,000 runs and took 2739 wickets, and his 14 'doubles' have been exceeded only by his soulmate Wilfred Rhodes. His 341 at Leicester in 1905 remains a Yorkshire record, and the county's gratitude was shown in a 1904 benefit of £3703 and a subsequent presentation of £738 after the war. He later became coach at Eton. He played 24 times for England with mixed success

7. Albert Knight, a thoughtful, well-read, religious man, was a conspicuous figure among professionals. He showed his true worth at the age of 26, and went with Warner's team to Australia in 1903–04, making a vital 70 not out in the decisive Sydney Test. He excelled in the square-drive, and later passed on the benefit of his experience as coach at Highgate School and Belvedere College, Dublin

continued next page

8. **R. S. Lucas**, who took the first English touring team to West Indies, in 1894–95. An amateur batsman for Middlesex throughout the 1890s, he added 338 with T. C. O'Brien for the fifth wicket at Hove in June, 1895, and for Old Merchant Taylors' he once hit seven balls out of the Charterhouse Square ground, two in succession through the same window of a house. He was a hockey international

9. **Ted Arnold**, who took a wicket with his first ball in a Test (Trumper, Sydney, 1903). He helped 'make' Worcestershire cricket, bowling fast-medium from a considerable height and batting well enough to secure the 'double' several times and twice making a double-century. His stand of 393 with amateur all-rounder W. B. Burns at Edgbaston in 1909 remains an English fifth-wicket record

10. **Percy Perrin**, a heavily-built Essex batsman, would have played for England but for his cumbersome fielding. Between 1896 and 1928 he made 29,709 runs, with 66 centuries, one of them, 343 not out (68 fours) against Derbyshire in 1904, remaining a county record. He later became a Test selector

11. **Arnold Warren**, who dismissed Trumper twice in his solitary Test match. A fast bowler of wavering moods, he sometimes wrought havoc for Derbyshire with his breakback ball, and at other times he looked ordinary. At Ashby-de-la-Zouch in 1912 he demolished Leicestershire after, it is said, spending his lunchtime in the beer-tent

12. **Arthur Fielder**, Kent's principal fast bowler for a dozen years before the war. He played six times against Australia, featuring in a frenzied one-wicket victory at Melbourne; for Kent against Worcestershire in 1909 he put on 235 for the last wicket with Frank Woolley. Most prominent among his feats was his 10 for 90 for Players v Gentlemen at Lord's in 1906. He owed much to Kent's deft slips fieldsmen

Canterbury on a warm day, with Hutchings and Woolley batting in their usual beautiful manner, was a vision of cricketing Heaven. Here Hutchings is bowled for 18 by D. M. Evans of Hampshire in August 1911. He made a century in the second innings of a drawn match. His partner in the photograph is Frank Woolley, who went on to make 108. Two other hundreds were made in this match – both by C. B. Fry, who complained at one point when 'Charlie' Blythe was tossing the ball high into the sun, blinding the batsman. *Top picture* shows the spectators stretching their legs during the luncheon interval

HAYES CATCHES LORD HAWKE

THE YORKSHIRE CAPTAIN IN CHARACTERISTIC ATTITUDE

THE CROWD ENCROACH UPON THE ARENA. APTED TO THE RESCUE

GEORGE HIRST PLAYS A GREAT GAME FOR YORKSHIRE

KNOX LIMPING PAINFULLY BACK TO HIS MARK

HUNTER'S WELL JUDGED CATCH THAT DISMISSED HOBBS

WITH THE GAME A TIE, THE CROWD BREAK ON TO THE FIELD. HAIGH SOLVES THE DIFFICULTY BY BOWLING A WIDE AND

HAYWARD AND HAYES STRUGGLE BACK TO THE PAVILION

About 80,000 people watched play during the three days of the 1906 Surrey v Yorkshire match, awarded to Walter Lees as a benefit. Some excellent cricket was played before Surrey completed a nine-wicket victory with 50 minutes to spare, Hirst making 87, Rhodes 53, and Tunnicliffe two half-centuries for the northern county and Hayward, Hayes and Crawford scoring well for Surrey, for whom Neville Knox, a terrifying fast bowler, took ten wickets. The beneficiary took seven. The central drawing is of Sam Apted, who for years prepared perfect batting wickets at The Oval

Top: August, 1911, and Sussex are heavily outgunned by Kent, who win by an innings at Hove after declaring with only three wickets down (Humphreys 191, Woolley 108 not out, Seymour 83). Here the Sussex captain, H. P. Chaplin, comes forward to a ball from D. W. Carr, a googly bowler playing his first match of the season for Kent. Two years earlier, when aged 37, Carr caused a sensation with his newly-acquired bowling method (he was originally a fast-medium bowler) and was selected for the Oval Test against Australia. In this his only appearance for England he took three important wickets straightaway, but MacLaren overbowled him and he finished with 7 for 282 off 69 overs in the match. In his remarkable first-class career of only six years Carr took 334 wickets at 16.84. *Bottom:* E. H. Killick, a diminutive, bespectacled left-hander who played in 389 successive matches for Sussex from 1898, places a ball from Woolley to leg. He made 42 and 70 in this forlorn contest

Thursday, July 27, 1911 was a great day for 20-year-old Middlesex googly bowler J. W. ('Young Jack') Hearne. Against Essex at Lord's he took 6 for 17, including a hat-trick, to send the opposition packing for a mere 78. Tarrant made 168 for Middlesex, supported by half-centuries from Warner, Hendren and Murrell, and Tarrant's 6 for 38 on a storm-dampened pitch brought an innings victory on the third day. The photograph is of Perrin, deceived and bowled by Hearne. *Below:* The Kent–Hampshire match at Canterbury in 1911 was more a batsman's than a bowler's match (refer page 51). Arthur Fielder, Kent's No. 1 fast bowler for so many seasons, appeals in vain for a catch at the wicket against the steady Alec Bowell, whose partner, Fry, shows that white sunhats are no particular fad of the nuclear age

3
DISTINGUISHED PERSONAGES

Miss Delamode (of Belgravia). " Well, dear, I must be off.   Don't you love Lord's ? "

Miss Dowdesley (of Far-West Kensingtonia). " I'm sure I should, only——" (*immersed in her own dreams*)—" We don't know any ! "

Reproduced by kind permission of Punch

Alfred Lyttelton (left, with Arthur Balfour, Prime Minister and brother-in-law) was a wicketkeeper-batsman (and sometime lob bowler) for Eton, Cambridge, Middlesex, Worcestershire, the Gentlemen, and England. Business at the Bar and in politics took him from the first-class game after 1887, though he took on the presidency of MCC in 1898. A superb tennis and rackets player, he also played football for England, and stood for all that was admirable in a sportsman. After dismissal by a lightning piece of stumping by Lancashire professional Dick Pilling he sought out the wicketkeeper after play and pressed £1 into his hand with a word of congratulation. He was perhaps the most distinguished member of a highly distinguished family, youngest of eight brothers. He became a bencher of the Inner Temple in 1899 and QC in 1900, and was successively legal private secretary to Sir Henry James (Attorney-General), Recorder of Hereford, Recorder of Oxford, and Chancellor of the Diocese of Rochester. He entered Parliament in 1895 as Member for Leamington, and was Colonial Secretary from 1903 to 1905. Yet in popular memory he is recalled as the wicketkeeper who took off his pads in a Test match at The Oval in 1884 and took 4 for 19 with underarm lobs. All eleven England players bowled in that Australian innings of 551. Cricket may have caused Lyttelton's death, in 1913, at the age of 56. He scored 89 in a match against Bethnal Green Tradesmen – Tom Hayward played, too, three days before making his hundredth century – and a blow from the ball caused an internal abscess. He died, after an operation, eleven days later, having whispered to one of his brothers, 'Don't let them make too much of the cricket ball – just a piece of bad luck'

The cricket world knew him as K. S. Ranjitsinhji – or 'Run-get-Sinhji' as *Punch* preferred, which was more precise than a Cockney's forlorn call from the terraces to 'Ramsgate Jimmy'. At Cambridge, fellow undergraduates settled for 'Smith', but to the vast majority he was known affectionately as 'Ranji'. He sits (front, nearest camera) atop the elephant on the way to his installation as Jam Saheb of the State of Nawanagar (3791 square miles) in India. The date is March 10, 1907, and at 34, though there is much cricket left in him and his glittering record cries out teasingly for extension, Ranji turns to the cause which has absorbed his senses through years of dispute. Bedecked in silk, jewels and pearls, he and his procession, much of it riding in borrowed carriages, risked the disease-ridden and foul-smelling streets of Jamnagar to the old palace, where, in his speech, Ranji, deeply conscious of his obligations to the 400-year-old throne, said, 'I shall endeavour to play the game so as not to lose whatever credit I have gained in another field.' After surviving an attack of typhoid he returned to English cricket in 1908, a wealthy nabob anxious to repay past kindnesses, with much interest, and in Nawanagar he proceeded to transform a crumbling economy into a state of relative pride and prosperity. He served in the Great War, seeing action at Neuve Chapelle but suffering badly from asthma and bronchitis. Then, while on leave in 1915, he lost his right eye in a shooting accident at Filey. He never revealed the name of the companion whose misplaced shot caused the injury. Full with the years, he played a handful of games for Sussex in 1920, and thenceforth was seen in such diverse places as his kingdom, rented homes in Staines and Ireland, the League of Nations assembly, and in his box at Lord's

A heavyweight gathering of prominent men at Cumberland Lodge, Windsor in June 1911, when Prince Albert of Schleswig-Holstein's XI played Charterhouse. The young man with cane and boater is the Prince of Wales (later King Edward VIII), who had been invested as a Knight of the Garter at Windsor Castle only hours earlier. He met W. G. Grace (white beard flowing) earlier than expected as the Champion had fallen to a slip catch third ball without scoring. Prince Albert of Schleswig-Holstein stands with hands behind back and Prince Christian of Schleswig-Holstein, a son-in-law of the late Queen Victoria, is on the right

From Hove to Hollywood: C. Aubrey Smith, known to millions of cinemagoers for his roles in *The Prisoner of Zenda, Little Lord Fauntleroy, Clive of India, The House of Rothschild, Trader Horn, The Hurricane, Lives of a Bengal Lancer*, etcetera, had earlier made his name on the stage, acting with such giants as Forbes Robertson, Sir Charles Hawtrey, Ellen Terry, Mrs Patrick Campbell, Billie Burke, and Ethel Barrymore. His taste for the theatre developed during his days at Cambridge, but for several years he was one of the most successful amateur cricketers, playing for Sussex on and off from 1882 to 1896. In 1887–88 he captained Shaw and Shrewsbury's team in Australia, and a year later led England in the first Test match ever against South Africa, at Port Elizabeth, taking 5 for 19 and 2 for 42 with left-arm medium-pace bowling that earned him the sobriquet 'Round the Corner' Smith for his peculiar approach to the wicket. Staying in South Africa for a time, he captained Transvaal in the first-ever Currie Cup match. He was knighted in 1944 for his contribution to Anglo–American relations, and for many years inspired a cricket community in Hollywood. He died in 1948, aged 85

Authors at play: *Above* – J. M. Barrie (left), most famous for *Peter Pan*, which was first performed at Christmas 1904, and *The Admirable Crichton*, was obsessed by cricket but was untalented at it. 'I bowl so slow,' he once said, 'that if, after I have delivered a ball and don't like the look of it, I can run after it and bring it back!' He formed his own team, the Allahakbarries (allegedly Moorish for 'God help us'), and played some hilarious 'Test matches' with literary cronies. In the striped blazer is Shan F. Bullock. *Below, left:* E. W. Hornung, creator of Raffles, the upper-class cricketer/burglar. *Right:* Sir Arthur Conan Doyle (facing camera), a good batsman but remembered, of course, for Sherlock Holmes and excursions into spiritualism

Parliament at play: The House of Commons team at the turn of the century, captained by John Burns, MP (seated, centre), whose brother was a fine MCC and Essex all-rounder. Back row – umpire, H. J. Reckitt, MP, A. G. Giles, V. A. Titchmarsh, umpire; seated – Hon. G. Verney, W. Younger, MP, Burns, J. Pease, MP, J. Dickson Poynder, MP

A treasury of literary personalities gathers for a carefree cricket match at Downe House in 1913. Back row – George Llewellyn Davies (adopted son of J. M. Barrie, Eton XI 1911–12, killed at Voormezeele, 1915, aged 21), T. L. Gilmour, Will Meredith, George Meredith jnr, Denis Mackail, Harry Graham, Dr Goffe; seated – A. A. Milne, Maurice Hewlett, J. M. Barrie, George Morrow, E. V. Lucas, Walter Frith; front – Percy Lucas, Audrey Lucas, T. Wrigley, Charles Tennyson, Willie Winter. *Below:* The face of destiny, seated second from the left, peers solemnly from the St Paul's School First XI group of 1906. It is 18-year-old opening batsman Bernard Law Montgomery, one day to become one of Britain's greatest army commanders, Viscount Montgomery of Alamein. He had a beautiful cover-drive, and in his sole encounter with old WG, when the school played London County, he 'hooked his slows to the boundary with great persistency'

A royal cricketer: Prince Christian Victor, elder son of Victoria and Albert's third daughter, Helena. He was a good wicketkeeper at Wellington College, but was kept out of the Oxford side by Hylton Philipson, who went on to play for England. He played hardly any first-class cricket (for I Zingari), but scored consistently well in army matches between duties in India (205 for the King's Royal Rifles v the Devonshire Regiment at Rawalpindi in 1893) and with the Green Jackets at Winchester and Dover. His endeavour to get up a match at Coomassie during the Ashanti Expedition was thwarted only because no bat or ball could be found! A popular and charming man, he died of enteric fever in 1900 (having escaped a shellburst on a rock nearby him) while serving in the Boer War, and was buried in Pretoria. He was 33. His statue stands outside the walls of Windsor Castle

Actors v Jockeys – a riotous mixture. Back row: G. P. Huntley, E. Mathews, H. Woodland, W. Dollery, D. Maher, H. Forsyth, J. Cannon, Ford Hamilton, W. H. Dawes, F. Blackman, V. O'Connor, Rutland Barrington, Hon. R. Beresford; seated: George Williamson, J. A. E. Malone, M. Cannon, George Edwardes; front: P. Chaloner, J. Blakeley, Robert Evett, F. Hunt, J. H. Martin, George Graves, K. Cannon, T. Cannon jnr, F. Hardy

An historic visit: King George V becomes the first sovereign to watch play in a Test match. It is July 16, 1912, and curiously the match, at Lord's, features Australia and South Africa, not England. The Triangular Tournament between the three countries was not a great success. Australia sent a weakened side after the withdrawal of the 'Big Six' following a dispute with the Board, the South Africans were hardly a strong combination, the weather was unkind, and many cricket-followers regarded the Tests as an unwelcome interference with the domestic programme. His Majesty saw South Africa batting, backs to the wall, and met both teams

The young princes, like their father, had but a passing interest in cricket, but the earnest endeavours of the schoolboys from Eton and Harrow were as likely to appeal to the sailor-suited boys as any of their seniors and betters. The MCC president's box at Lord's at least offered all the comforts

The young Princes in the President's box.

4
CLUB CRICKET

Mitcham Green by Lucien Davis

A blaze of blazers at Raeburn Place, Edinburgh in July 1900, when the Grange Cricket Club played host to the Authentics. Back row – H. D. Corbet, E. Britten-Holmes, C. D. Fisher, F. H. Latham, R. S. Darling; middle row – A. M. Hollins, C. J. L. Boyd, B. J. T. Bosanquet, J. S. Munn, F. Hunter, F. G. Robinson, T. Johnston; seated – R. H. Johnston, T. H. K. Dashwood, L. M. Balfour-Melville, F. H. Hollins, A. G. G. Asher, H. W. Kaye, D. L. A. Smith

Tally ho! We're off to the match! Players from the Lyndhurst club travel to the match at Lymington in style . . . so long as the weather stays fine. *Below:* In September 1908 a granite column commemorating the eighteenth-century glories of the Hambledon club was unveiled, and a match played between teams styled 'Hambledon' and 'An England XI', the former winning a three-day match by five wickets. Phil Mead, then only 21, stands to the left of the column, C. B. Fry is in white, with Capt E. G. Wynyard next to him (striped blazer)

Charles Absolon, the Grand Old Man of London club cricket, pictured on his ninetieth birthday, on May 30, 1907, less than a year before his death. He played until he was 80, and actually took 209 wickets when he was 76. He remembered playing on Queen Victoria's Coronation Day, June 28, 1838, for Butchers against Bakers at Wallingford, and participated in every game he could find – sometimes two in a day – for 71 years, bowling old-fashioned underarm lobs and making his share of runs. In the last 30 years he took 8500 wickets and scored 26,000 runs, and his output in the preceding 41 years can only be guessed at. He played with E. M. and W. G. Grace when they were schoolboys, and enjoyed telling of his successes against some of the eminent players of his day, and of playing against four successive generations of the Bentley family. A testimonial match at The Oval raised £120 for him in 1896. A final absurd statistic from his remarkable record: he did the hat-trick 59 times between 1871 and 1893

Probably the strongest genuine club side of all time was Hampstead in the 1890s. In this group there are five men who played for Middlesex plus four who had played or were to play Test cricket: F. R. 'Demon' Spofforth (Australia) (seated sixth from left), Andrew Stoddart (next to him, also in straw boater), Gregor MacGregor (on ground, extreme left), and L. J. Moon (on ground, fifth from left). Fourth from the right, on the ground, is the father of photographer Sir Cecil Beaton

The Wanderers (founded as Clapham Wanderers by Stanley Colman, scorer of over a hundred centuries in non-first-class cricket and cousin of the 'Mustard Millionaire'), pictured during their 1909 tour of Kent and Sussex. Back row – P. P. Lincoln, F. W. Robarts, Dr H. C. Pretty, J. N. Crawford, R. T. Crawford, P. H. Slater, N. Leicester-Clarke, R. Kenward; seated – A. M. Latham, S. Colman, D. L. A. Jephson, R. B. Brooks. Jack Crawford had already played for England, and Jephson was for years a valuable batsman and lob bowler for Surrey. There were other first-class players in this side, but Slater took the tour honours with innings of 197 and 145 not out

'Caught at the Wicket' – as the shadows lengthen on another summer's afternoon of club cricket somewhere in England in the sixth decade of the reign of Victoria. The umpire is hardly in an ideal position

Contrast in style and spirit – the Free Foresters (above), founded in 1856 and originally an intimate cricket club for gentlemen from the Midlands, and northern league cricket (*below*), unpretentious, uncompromising, unglamorous. The Foresters pictured beat Oxford University in 1906, Wynyard and Kortright scoring centuries, Cobbold taking 11 for 135 and Simpson-Hayward 5 for 59 with underarm lobs. The players are: back row – C. J. Kortright, R. V. Buxton, G. H. Simpson–Hayward, H. Martyn; seated – H. A. Arkwright, Capt. E. G. Wynyard, E. C. Mordaunt, S. M. J. Woods, R. E. Foster; front – H. F. Wright, P. W. Cobbold. The league match, at Accrington, Lancashire, with Church the visitors, has drawn a typically large and eager audience of men who, it has been said, might otherwise have needed prising out of the pub by 'the missis'. The competitive games produced prompt starts, positive play, and the keenest competition

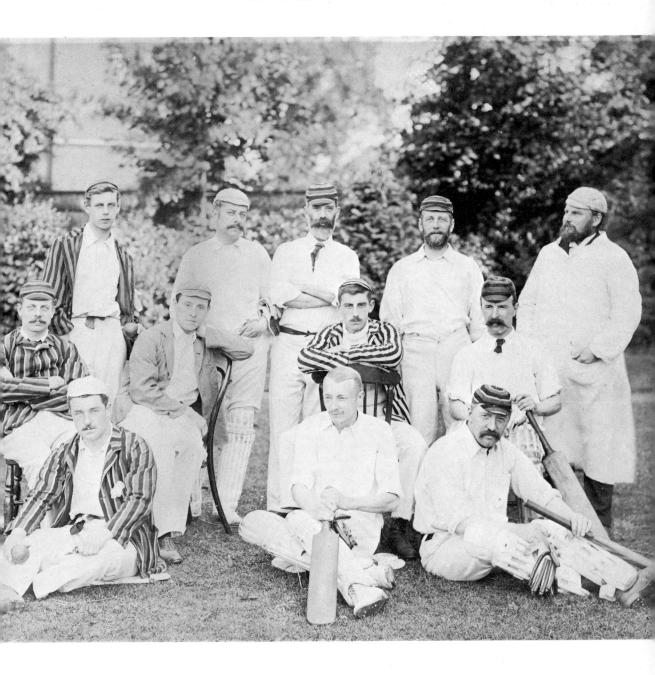

An unidentified team group of the 1890s, taken by the fashionable photographers Elliott & Fry of Baker Street. The picture might have looked more of an antique in the 1960s than it does today, when moustaches, beards and shorter hair are in fashion. What was passing through those twelve minds as they waited for the man beneath the camera cape to do his work? Is my bad trot with the bat about to end? Will the bank manager foreclose on me, as threatened? What did the skipper think of that ripping off-drive of mine? I wonder if Emily will say yes this evening?

Meopham Cricket Club, in Kent, celebrated their bicentenary in 1976, and were already over a century old when this picture was taken in 1893. Back row– A. Wellard, W. Coombes, J. Wellard, C. Taylor, J. Dyke, H. Snape, G. Holland; middle – W. Ashdown, P. Coombes, A. Dryland, Rev. V. Batson, R. French; front – C. Coombes, J. Day. An entry in the club accounts for 1903 shows: Hire of horse, 6 days rolling @ 5/0d – £1/10/0d. Man with horse, 6 days rolling @ 3/6d – £1/1/0d. *Below:* Three prominent Yorkshire club cricketers of the 1890s – left to right, William Fletcher, of Low Moor and Leeds, who played a few matches for the county, doing the hat-trick against MCC at Lord's; T. Midgley, of Moortown; H. Walshaw, of Hunslet. The senior clubs in Yorkshire have always provided a steady stream of talent for the county club

5
ON
COLONIAL AND FOREIGN
FIELDS

The oldest series of international cricket matches is between the USA and Canada, begun in 1844. This photograph of both teams in the 1905 contest, at Rosedale, Toronto, includes some lastingly famous North American cricketers – W. P. O'Neill and E. M. Cregar (both in striped blazers, back row), J. B. King, the great swing-bowling all-rounder (seated fourth from left), and C. C. Morris (on ground, extreme right). Canada won by an innings and 29 runs. *Below:* Sydney Cricket Ground, with the Australians taking the field during one of the 1903–04 Test matches against England. The Hill on the far side has yet to be crowned with the huge, informative scoreboard, and the ground is encircled by a cycle track, laid in 1896 and taken up in 1921

The Queen's Park ground, Port of Spain, Trinidad in the 1890s, with tennis court markings on the outfield. Many a gripping inter-island and Test match has been played here in this picturesque setting, an amphitheatre of wooded hills. *Below:* A matting wicket at Cape Town. Much of South Africa's senior cricket was played on this kind of artificial surface until well into the twentieth century

In April 1891 Kimberley sent a side down to Johannesburg ('a terrible journey') to play Transvaal in the second Currie Cup competition. Played before wildly enthusiastic crowds, the match lasted a week and resulted unexpectedly in a win for Kimberley, whose captain, A. B. Tancred, 'South Africa's WG' (seated behind trophy), scored 89 and 62. C. E. Finlason (behind Tancred) made 154 not out, and J. H. Piton (in blazer and cap, beside trophy), an underarm bowler, took 13 for 204 in the match. *Below:* The Ramblers Club, Bloemfontein, Orange Free State, an imposing sports complex founded in the 1890s. During the Boer War it was transformed into a military hospital under the control of Dr Conan Doyle, and was soon an obscene den of raging typhoid, infested with flies. By the Heavenly gesture of a lightning strike three years later the original buildings were burned down

Five prominent Melbourne cricketers early this century: from left – Bill Bruce, Hugh Trumble, Vernon Ransford, Gerry Hazlitt, Warwick Armstrong (in cap). All played for their country

Above, right: Frank Laver, who went on to play for and manage Australian teams, and was also an explorer and photographer, shown after his 352 not out in 1892–93 for the East Melbourne club against St Kilda. *Below:* The ladies and gentlemen of Cleveland (Ohio) Cricket Club, who played each other before the First War. The gentlemen, handicapped by having to bat left-handed with broomsticks, not surprisingly lost

Kensington Oval, Bridgetown, Barbados, a small ground with an eventful future awaiting it. The United Kingdom flag flies confidently in the breeze as Lord Hawke's amateur side play the locals. *Below:* The Dutch team which played against Belgium, France, and MCC in a festival in Brussels to celebrate the Exhibition of 1910. Back row – G. Alpen (umpire), W. Eigeman, P. de Groot, P. Aernouts, C. van Loon, W. Gerke, H. van Booven, W. W. Whelan (umpire); seated – C. Feith, J. H. Hisgen, J. C. Schröder, C. J. Posthuma, W. van Waveren

The Consolidated Goldfields and Corner House cricket teams grouped in Johannesburg in 1904, with distinguished visitor Lord Harris (seated, centre). Two eminent South African Test cricketers here are Aubrey Faulkner, the Corner House captain (two to the right of Lord Harris) and E. A. Halliwell (extreme right). *Below:* Melbourne Cricket Ground in the 1890s, barely recognisable if compared against the modern reconstructed stadium developed for the 1956 Olympic Games. The park outside remains but the parkland atmosphere of the ground where the first-ever Test match was played, in 1877, has gone forever

Almost a fashion parade of hats at Adelaide Oval in the early 1900s, where some of the ladies would appear to
have as little interest in the cricket as the dog in the foreground. People travelled sometimes for days to reach the
cities when big matches, particularly Tests, were played. Great nation in the making Australia may have been, but
even then those with sporting interests – and that meant a majority – insisted on getting the proper priorities
worked out for their business and leisure routines

C Squadron 16th Lancers, who won the Regimental Cup in India in 1898. The contemporary caption stated: 'Most of the above group have since fallen in South Africa. The 16th (Queen's) Lancers is the only British cavalry regiment that has ever broken an infantry square in battle'. *Below:* The Caribbean island of St Vincent receives an English team in 1897, the crowd colourfully dressed and excitable. One straight-drive by 'Plum' Warner knocked a tray full of cakes clean off the head of a black woman standing near the ropes. The crossing from Grenada, in a 170-ton vessel, had been 'terrible', and the English players looked pale and seedy upon arrival. Worse followed: accommodation shortage forced them to sleep two to a bed in Mrs Brisbane's hotel, and most of the players were bitten from feet to forehead by mosquitoes, who, with astounding discretion, left Lord Hawke alone

The first cricket team to represent New Zealand (against New South Wales at Christchurch, February 1894). Back row – A. M. Ollivier (selector), I. Mills, H. De Maus, J. C. Lawton, T. D. Condell (umpire); middle row – R. W. Barry (scorer), J. D. Lawrence, A. R. Holdship (captain), L. A. Cuff, J. N. Fowke, C. Gore, W. H. Wynn-Williams (Canterbury Cricket Association president); front – A. M. Labatt, E. V. Palmer, W. Robertson. It was not until 1978 that New Zealand achieved their first victory in a Test match against England, having beaten Australia for the first time in 1974

Thomas Patrick Horan, born in Middleton, County Cork and taken to Australia as a youngster, played fifteen times for his adopted country, captaining in two Tests won heavily by England. He became a popular cricket-writer for *The Australasian* under the pen-name 'Felix'. As a batsman he evidently felt that appearances counted for little and that batting gloves were for 'softies'

6
HOUSEHOLD
NAMES

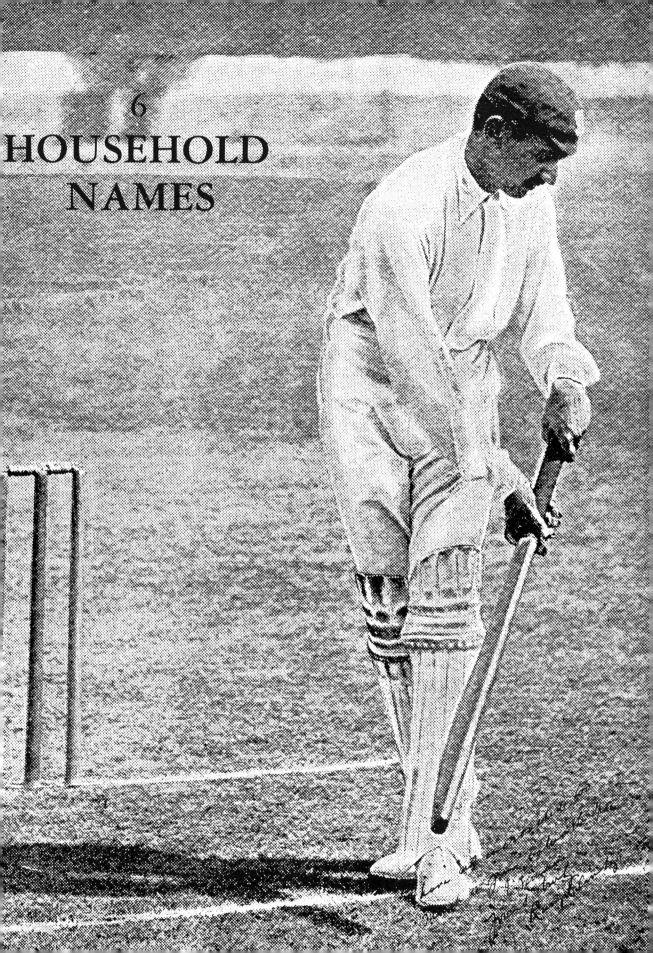

The players who brought Surrey the Championship in 1892, for the third year running: back row – Tom Richardson, E. C. Streatfeild, K. J. Key, Maurice Read, Fred Boyington (scorer); seated – Harry Wood, George Lohmann, John Shuter (captain), Walter Read, Bill Lockwood; front – Bobby Abel, Robert Henderson. Nine counties only were in the County Championship, and Surrey won thirteen of their sixteen matches, with Lockwood and Lohmann each taking over 100 wickets and W. W. Read making the only three centuries for the side. Only one century was scored against them

Few batting records have survived eighty-odd years, but one which has is the Somerset first-wicket record of 346 made in 1892 by L. C. H. Palairet (146), a supreme stylist, and H. T. Hewett (201), a ferocious left-hander who captained the side. They hit up 78 in three-quarters of an hour on the first evening and on the second day the Yorkshire bowlers, who included Jackson, Peel, and Wainwright, were put to the sword. Somerset (592) led by 293 on the second evening, but Taunton was a very rainy place on the last day, a Saturday, and no further play was possible

Defiant, imperious, aware of both his appearance and his importance, Archie MacLaren, captain of Lancashire and England, gives the photographer a view of himself similar to that 'enjoyed' by bowlers. He was fit enough at 51 to score a double-century during a tour of New Zealand

Above: In the spring of 1912 a Test trial was played at The Oval – not very well supported by the public to judge from the empty rows of seating. A very strong 'England' XI beat The Rest by an innings, but a redeeming performance for the vanquished was Kent's 'Punter' Humphreys' top-score in each innings. Here he plays a ball past Rhodes in the gully, with E. J. 'Tiger' Smith keeping wicket, Fry at square leg, Woolley at first slip, Frank Foster second, and Johnny Douglas the other batsman. A highlight of the match was a hattrick (Seymour, Hayward, Sharp) by S. F. Barnes. *Right:* Reginald Erskine 'Tip' Foster, one of the gods of cricket in the early 1900s. He made two centuries at Lord's in 1900 on his debut for Gentlemen v Players and once also made a pair of hundreds in the same match for Worcestershire as did his brother Wilfred

These immaculately-attired 'city-gents' are none other than the captains of ten of the counties in 1901: standing – D. L. A. Jephson (Surrey), G. L. Jessop (Gloucestershire), R. E. Foster (Worcestershire), S. M. J. Woods (Somerset), J. R. Mason (Kent); seated – G. MacGregor (Middlesex), H. W. Bainbridge (Warwickshire), H. G. Owen (Essex), Lord Hawke (Yorkshire), C. E. de Trafford (Leicestershire). Amateurs all, their care for the spirit in which the game was played was unquestionably greater than that of many of their present-day counterparts, who are preoccupied with avoiding defeat

Two of the finest left-handers the world has seen, both pictured in the flush of their youth. *Top:* Clem Hill, born in Adelaide in 1877, and maker of 3412 runs for Australia in his 49 Tests between 1896 and 1911–12. He was described by his senior team-mate George Giffen as a 'wonder', 'remarkably cool, self-possessed', though Giffen warned the youngster against overuse of the hook, 'his fancy stroke'. *Right:* Frank Woolley, born in Tonbridge in 1887 and second only to Hobbs with a career aggregate of 58,969 runs. His total of 1015 catches in a career stretching from 1906 to 1938 is a clear record, and in 64 appearances for England he made 3283 runs. When the photograph was taken nearly all of this lay ahead of the tall, willowy, young man

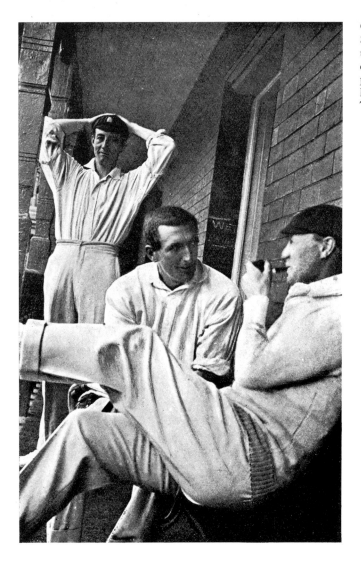

Conversation worth hearing: Reggie Spooner, hands on head, will be hearing the words of wit or wisdom being exchanged by Charles Fry and a pipe-puffing Gilbert Jessop during a hold-up in play during one of the 1912 Test matches

The tragic Johnny Briggs with his beloved twin sons. A slow-medium left-arm bowler who could tease and destroy, he went on six tours of Australia and one to South Africa, and took 118 wickets in Tests at only 17.74 apiece. Only 5ft 5in tall, he was a favourite not only in Lancashire, his adopted county. His highest score, 186 against Surrey at Aigburth, was made two days after his marriage in 1885. In 1899 he suffered a serious epileptic fit, but after eight months in an asylum he seemed to have recovered. But after only a further year he was obliged by a fresh breakdown to return to hospital, where he died ten months later

A. E. Knight, who often prayed before, during or after an innings, once prompting Lancashire fast bowler Walter Brearley, according to Neville Cardus, to report him to the MCC!

Bernard Bosanquet, the innovator. His googly caused fun and anguish, won many a match, and attracted disciples in all countries, though the dearth of English wrist-spinners today would doubtless have appalled 'Bosie' himself

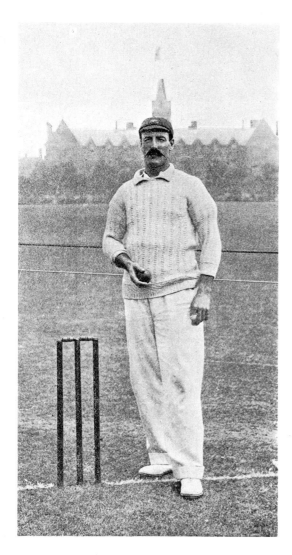

Ernie Jones, the rough-and-ready fast bowler from Australia who spearheaded the attack in the late 1890s, by way of an answer to England's Tom Richardson. After some tuition he became a well-co-ordinated bowler, keen on the bouncer, and very highly regarded by all of England's leading batsmen of his time. He recovered from being no-balled for throwing by Jim Phillips at Melbourne in the 1897–98 series

Ted Alletson, immortalised by one astonishing innings. A massive man with an arm-span of 6ft 6in, in May 1911 at Hove, going in number nine in Nottinghamshire's second innings, after a dip in the sea, he hit 189 off Sussex in 90 minutes, his last 142 in only 40 minutes, starting from the luncheon interval. At one point five balls were out of the ground – lost. Driving most of the time, he hit 'Tim' Killick for 22 in one over and 34 in another. The pavilion, the clock, the skating rink were all bombarded – and Alletson was batting with only one sound wrist

Above: Father had a tale to tell . . . two years later, when Fred Tate was blamed for England's defeat by Australia in 1902 at Old Trafford, where he dropped an outfield catch and was bowled, last man out, with England four runs from victory. The boy, Maurice, grew up to play for Sussex and England with great success. *Top right:* Douglas Ward Carr, the sensation of 1909, when, in his 38th year, after a lifetime of club cricket, chiefly with The Mote, Kent, he was chosen by the county and for the Gentlemen and finally by England for his newly-perfected leg-break/googly bowling. He took wickets for each of these teams, but at high cost in the Oval Test, where he was not used very shrewdly. His was an ephemeral but fascinating presence, like Alletson's. *Right:* A not-instantly-recognisable picture of Jack Hobbs, taken in 1905, when he was not yet 23, and in his first season with Surrey. 'He has all the makings of a really great cricketer,' wrote W. A. Bettesworth in *Cricket*

Albert Trott, who burst on the Test match scene in 1894–95 but was subsequently ignored by the Australian selectors. A hard hitter, an overwhelming fast-medium bowler, and a safe catcher with huge hands, he liked a pint, was easy-going, sometimes mischievous, but the victim later in life of the painful effects of dropsy, and ended it all with a pistol-shot in his lodgings at Willesden in August 1914, leaving his wardrobe to his landlady; the coroner found £4 in cash

Lofty William Gunn, 6ft 3in, and Arthur Shrewsbury, 5 ft 8 in, whose cultured batting brought so many runs for Nottinghamshire and England. They had three partnerships of over 300; their 398 for the second wicket against Sussex in 1890, at Trent Bridge, their spiritual home, remains the highest stand for the county. Gunn drove especially well, and must have resembled Tom Graveney in later years by his ease and sense of command. He played eleven times for England, making a century in the Manchester Test of 1893, and also played football against Scotland and Wales. A partner in the bat-making firm of Gunn & Moore, he died in 1921, a wealthy man. Of Shrewsbury little need be added to W. G. Grace's response to an enquiry as to the best batsman of the day – apart from himself, of course: 'Give me Arthur!'

Major E. G. ('Teddy') Wynyard, a professional soldier, was tall and powerful, excelling in the full-blooded drive and a hit through mid-on as he dropped onto his right knee. He played for Hampshire, sharing a surviving record of 411 for the sixth wicket with Major R. M. Poore at Taunton in 1899, and three times for England, though having to decline two Australian tours because of military commitments. He was also an expert figure-skater and tobogganist, and played football for England. Sometimes testy, he fell out with Ranjitsinhji when the young Indian inadvertently ate some of his grapes

Bobby Peel, whose dismissal by Yorkshire in 1897 came in a grotesque manner: he was the worse for drink, and urinated on the pitch, so it is said, giving Lord Hawke little option but to banish him. Yet this ought not to obscure a successful career in which he took 102 Test wickets, *all* against Australia, and had some worthy innings, including a double-century against Warwickshire in 1896, when Yorkshire made 887. His 6 for 67 (after having several teeth extracted) won a Sydney Test for England by ten runs, but even then his captain had had to sober him up under a cold shower

Another proud opening pair, 'Long John' Tunnicliffe and Jack Brown, Yorkshire's redoubtable professional numbers one and two in the 1890s, pictured after making 378 for the first wicket against Sussex at Bramall Lane in 1897. Tunnicliffe was out for 147 and Brown went on to 311. Declaring at 681 for 5, Yorkshire won by an innings and 307 runs, Wainwright scoring 104 not out and Milligan taking 12 for 110 in the match. Sussex avenged themselves in the return a month later at Brighton

It is given to few to have their names bestowed upon a cricket match, but Robert St Leger Fowler will be forever associated with the Eton v Harrow game of 1910. He captained Eton, who made only 67 to Harrow's 232 and were but four runs ahead, thanks to Fowler's 64, when the ninth wicket fell in the follow-on. The Hon. J. N. Manners (killed in the war) hit 40 not out, putting on 50 for the last wicket, and Harrow needed a mere 55 to win. Fowler, bowling accurate off-breaks on a soft Lord's pitch, then took 8 for 23 in 10 overs to bring his side a sensational nine-run victory. The Army later claimed him and he played hardly any first-class cricket

Above: Hirst and Rhodes, the most renowned pair in Yorkshire history. Both were born in the village of Kirkheaton, near Huddersfield, and both batted right-hand and bowled left- (Hirst fast swervers, Rhodes guileful slows). Between them they scored over 75,000 runs and took nearly 7000 wickets. Cricket truly was their lives, neither giving thought to retirement until well into his forties. *Right:* George Lohmann, of the confident gait, who learned the game on Wandsworth Common, and took over 1500 wickets for Surrey with extremely skilful medium-pace bowling which also brought him 112 Test wickets at the astoundingly low cost of 10.75 each, in 18 matches. Against South Africa in 1895–96 he took 8 for 7 at Port Elizabeth and 9 for 28 at Johannesburg, and at Sydney in 1886–87 he took eight Australian wickets for 35. Dogged by ill-health, he sought recovery in South Africa, but died there of tuberculosis in 1901, aged 36

Ranjitsinhji, one of the leading 'glamour boys' of the day, has a bit of a net, watched by a gathering of fortunates many of whom are of the gentler sex. *Below:* During Yorkshire's match against Notts at Headingley in July, 1908 a presentation of silverware was made to Lord Hawke (in cap) to mark his 25 years of captaincy. Lord Wharncliffe (speaking) referred to Hawke's 'firmness, unvarying courtesy, and sincere love of the game', and concluded: 'Lord Hawke and his fellow cricketers are doing great things for their country in showing that to lead a healthy life is to ensure steady nerve and all those qualities which every Englishman ought to have to be serviceable. . . . In the time of England's trouble, if it should come, would not they and their descendants be the most trustworthy men to play the game?'

Frank Foster, unrelated to the Worcestershire family of cricketers, had a meteoric career, first playing for Warwickshire in 1908, and leading them to their first Championship in 1911, when he was only 22. He contributed much personally that season, making a hundred in each of the Yorkshire matches and 200 against Surrey at Edgbaston, and completing the 'double'. He took 32 wickets for England that winter in a highly successful series in Australia, his fast left-arm swerve bowling proving a deadly complement to S. F. Barnes's great artistry, but the strain on such a young man showed in 1912. By 1914, having rested for a time, his free-stroking right-hand batting registered 305 not out against Worcestershire at Dudley (still the county record) and again he did the double. A brief but glorious career was brought to an end by a motor-cycle accident during the war

Mr. F. R. FOSTER
Captain Warwickshire Eleven
Champion County · Season 1911

Cricket owes much to George W. Beldam (1868–1937), the Middlesex batsman who took hundreds of action photographs of cricketers in the early 1900s. Here, in the Brighton sunshine, he is making more admirable plates for posterity, though those *below*, of Sussex's Australian W. L. Murdoch playing the eccentric 'dog-stroke', and (*bottom*) J. T. Hearne, prolific wicket-taker for Middlesex, in the final leap of his smooth and rhythmic action, were taken by the less well-known W. A. Rouch

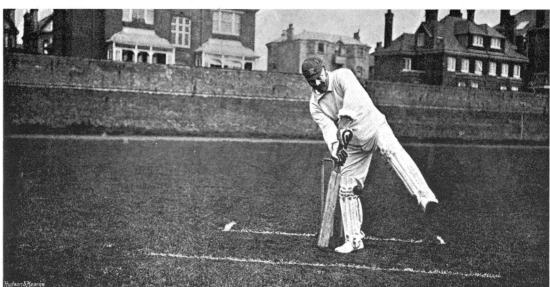

C. L. Townsend, who played for Gloucestershire at sixteen and had remarkable success with heavily-spun leg-breaks and vigorous left-hand batting in the late 1890s. In 1893 he did the hat-trick against Somerset per medium of three stumpings by W. H. Brain

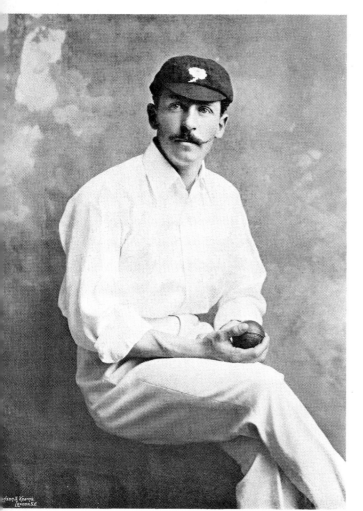 

Two lesser-known tragic figures: *Left* – Frank Milligan, a cavalier amateur all-rounder, schooled at Eton, a worthy contributor to the Gentlemen's fortunes against the Players, and sometimes brilliant performer for Yorkshire as impetuous batsman, erratic but often dangerous fast bowler, and dynamic fieldsman. He was killed in the Rhodesia Frontier Forces' attempt to relieve Mafeking. *Right* – Arthur Woodcock, a magnificent specimen of Midlands manhood whose speed was close to that of Kortright for a season or so. He helped the young Tom Richardson while playing for the Mitcham club, and did wonders as coach to Haverford College in America, returning to play for Leicestershire each summer. In 1910 he died from self-administered poison. He was 44

C. B. Fry has captioned this photo in his widely-acclaimed book *Batsmanship* (1912): 'A correctly played back-stroke'. Modern coaches will have a few thoughts on the separated hands and the flying left foot, but the method brought abundant success to this brilliant Englishman

'Plum' Warner lived at Caring House, near Maidstone, during the first decade of the century, and generated much cricket interest locally, once getting up a side which included the future Admiral Lord Jellicoe and playing against HMS *Dominion*, who fielded four future Commanders-in-Chief of Mediterranean, Atlantic, or Home Fleets. Here, in 1911, he relaxes at Caring with Patsy Hendren, who became a great Lord's favourite between the wars, F. L. Fane, captain of Essex and England, Esmond (son), Elizabeth (daughter) with Warner, Agnes (wife), and John Hendren

Frank Gillett's impressions of play in the Yorkshire v Rest of England match played as late as September 12–14 in 1901, for the benefit of the family of the late William Yardley, who was second only to W. G. Grace as a batsman in the early 1870s. Here at Lord's C. B. Fry scored his sixth successive century, a record since equalled only by Don Bradman and Mike Procter. Later in the innings G. L. Jessop completed a small matter of 233 in 2½ hours, his first double-century. Albert Trott enjoyed the match too, taking 5 for 86 and 8 for 84 against the champion county

Gilbert Laird Jessop (1874–1955), whose deeds fill 5½ pages of *MCC Cricket Scores and Biographies*, three of them listing his exceptionally fast-scoring innings, mainly for Gloucestershire. His hurricane, unorthodox batting often swung a match completely around in an hour or less

Crawford became a household name in the first-class cricket world in the 1900s, and half the cause was the Reverend J. C. 'Parson' Crawford, chaplain at Cane Hill Asylum, Surrey (where Charlie Chaplin's mother was several times a patient). A former Kent and Sussex player himself, 'Parson' was father of VFS, RT, and JN, all of whom became eminent county cricketers, Jack also playing for England

Cyril Foley played for Eton, Cambridge, and Middlesex either side of 1900, and wrote a chatty book of reminiscence, *Autumn Foliage*, which contained a description of his involvement in the abortive Jameson Raid outside Johannesburg in early January 1896. It also reveals a fascination towards the 'golden-hearted' W. G. Grace – and the way he said 'Glasstershire' and dropped an occasional 'h'

C. T. B. ('Charlie') Turner – 'The Terror' – had the almost unrivalled striking rate of 101 Test wickets (all English) in only 17 Tests for Australia. He took many in harness with the left-armer Jack Ferris. Practising at dawn as a youngster in Bathurst, NSW, where he was a stable-boy for Cobb & Co., he taught himself to bowl at varying paces and with varying off-break. In 1895 he became one of the earliest of Test cricketers to be discarded summarily while there was still much good cricket left in him

Household names in late Victorian and Edwardian American cricket were the Newhalls of Philadelphia. In 190?
an eleven of Newhalls played against Baltimore. Pictured are: top three – C. Stevenson Newhall, Charles A
Newhall, Harrison L. Newhall; six in middle row – Robert S. Newhall, Cushman Newhall, Thomas Newhall
Dan S. Newhall, George M. Newhall, Walter S. Newhall; four in front – D. Allerton Newhall, William P
Newhall, Morton L. Newhall, David Newhall. Charles had been a very successful fast bowler for USA in matche
against English and Australian representative sides, and Walter was the best American batsman of his time
succeeded in that reputation by Robert. The younger members of the family were, apart from William P., unable
to match the consistent performances of the previous generations

Above: Bill Lockwood, who, like many a true all-rounder, would have made many more runs but for his exertions as a bowler. He had a lovely off-drive, left foot thrown to the pitch of the ball, as this picture suggests. The highest of his fifteen centuries was 165 against Leicestershire at The Oval in 1900. *Right:* David Hunter, who succeeded his brother Joe (who died in 1891, aged only 34) as Yorkshire's wicketkeeper and achieved 920 catches and 352 stumpings between 1888 and 1909, when he was 49. Tall, Scarborough-born, he had the duty and privilege of keeping wicket to Hirst and Rhodes and Peel and Haigh, and away from the game he amused himself with bell-ringing, clog-dancing, weightlifting and breeding canaries

Once upon a time, in Malvern, Worcestershire, a clergyman named Henry Foster produced seven sons, and they all played cricket for the county. One of them scored 287 in his first Test match for England, and several of them excelled also at other sports. It is no fairytale. Worcestershire for a time was referred to as 'Fostershire'. Gathered around their sire, anti-clockwise from top left, are Reginald, Wilfred, Maurice, Johnny, Geoffrey, Harry, and Basil. Johnny, the youngest, was the last survivor, dying in 1978

Frank Field, of Warwickshire, who earned his captain's undying affection by taking 122 wickets at 19.48, with stout-hearted fast bowling, to play a major part in the county's first Championship. In his only appearance for the Players against the Gentlemen (Scarborough, 1911) he took 8 for 94, his haul including Spooner, Douglas, Faulkner, Warner, Hutchings, and Jessop

The 1909 season ended in sawdust and dampness. At The Oval in mid-September, champion county Kent played a Rest of England XI, and Frank Woolley (pictured) made an uncomfortable 19 before being bowled by Buckenham, the Essex fast bowler. Here (large picture) he is dropped by Albert Relf at fine gully, with Tarrant (slip) and Oates (wicketkeeper) watching the accident. In the top smaller picture he has been dropped off a sharp return to Buckenham, and in the lower one he is having yet another reprieve at the erring hands of Oates. Woolley seldom left a match empty-handed, however, and in this game he had already secured the illustrious wicket of Hobbs

No bowler has yet approached Hugh Trumble's 141 wickets in England v Australia Test matches. He played in 32 matches for Australia between 1890 and 1904, touring England five times, and took a hat-trick at Melbourne in the 1901–02 series and again in the 1903–04 series. Son of an Irishman and his Scottish wife, Trumble was well over six feet tall, and bowled a deceptive and accurate medium-pace ball, to an off field, with a pronounced off-break. He was also a very fine slip fielder and useful batsman. From 1911 until his death in 1938 he was a popular secretary of Melbourne Cricket Club

An all-rounder in the fullest sense, Jim Phillips, born in Adelaide, tried his luck in England around 1888 and for a number of years was on the ground staff at Lord's and played for Middlesex. Often he returned to Australia in the winter, so having cricket all the year, but whatever he may have achieved with his slowish roundarm bowling it was as nothing beside his contribution as a first-class umpire, for his resolute approach halted the spread of suspect bowling actions. He no-balled Ernest Jones, C. B. Fry and Mold for throwing – and each on his respective home ground. He coached in New Zealand; he acted as manager, umpire, reporter and talent scout on Stoddart's team's 1897–98 tour of Australia; he made money later as a mining engineer in North America; and he died in Vancouver in 1930. It is regrettable that 'Dimboola Jim' never found time for an autobiography

Another busy sportsman was Frank Mitchell, Yorkshire-born, triple Blue at Cambridge, England rugby forward, Test batsman for England against South Africa, and captain of South Africa against England and Australia in three of the 1912 Triangular Tests, having become secretary to Sir Abe Bailey in the Transvaal. Yet history tends to remember him chiefly as the Cambridge captain who in 1896 instructed his fast bowler E. B. Shine to give away extras to deny Oxford the compulsory follow-on. Members stood up and shouted 'Play the game!' and one threw his field-glasses at Mitchell. Four years later the follow-on became optional

Upon his retirement as Yorkshire's captain after 28 years, Lord Hawke, now 50, entertained the team at his home, Wighill Park, Tadcaster. His famous remark 'Pray God no professional shall ever captain England' has often been misunderstood: he deeply admired good professionals, but felt their attitude towards the game made them unsuitable for command. Pictured are: back row – J. Hoyland, W. Rhodes, M. W. Booth, Major J. M. Dawson, J. T. Newstead; standing – E. J. Radcliffe, B. B. Wilson, Hon. H. Hawke, Hon. Miss Mary Hawke, T. L. Taylor, D. Denton, Hon. Miss Alice Hawke, F. C. Toone, W. H. Swaine, R. W. Frank, D. Hunter, A. Drake; seated – Hon. Miss E. Hawke, Mrs E. J. Radcliffe, C. Stokes, Lady Hawke, Rev. E. S. Carter, Mrs T. L. Taylor, G. H. Hirst, Miss M. Wintour; front – S. Haigh, W. E. Bates, H. Watson, Lord Hawke, W. H. Wilkinson, J. T. Rothery, A. Dolphin, H. Myers. *Right:* David Denton, a powerful, game hitter, reputed, a little unfairly, to have been the luckiest of batsmen when it came to dropped catches. The fact remains that he scored 33,000 runs for Yorkshire, with 61 centuries, and played eleven times for England when the country seemed to be bristling with great batsmen

The fitness and relative agility demanded of first-class cricketers in today's game would probably preclude the participation of someone as comfortably-built as Harry Baldwin, who took hundreds of wickets for Hampshire with slow-medium off-breaks, and appeared to enjoy every moment of his career

Francis Gilbertson Justice Ford, 'Six-foot-two of don't-care', youngest and best of a brotherhood, and extremely forceful left-hand bat – along Woolley lines – for Repton, Cambridge, Middlesex, the Gentlemen, and England. Woe betide any fieldsman who stood in the line of his best drives, cuts and hooks. He was sometimes called 'Stork', for reasons made obvious by the photograph

George Thompson, a clever fast-medium bowler and fine batsman, had much to do with Northamptonshire's elevation to first-class status in 1905, and went on to play for England six times. He had already taken 199 wickets at seven each on the non-Test tour of New Zealand and Australia in 1902–03. 'The Northampton Nugget's' service, with Bill East's, put their county on the cricket map

7
THE NATIONAL GAME

PRECEDENCE AT BATTERSEA:
" Garn !   The treasurer goes in before the bloomin' seckertary ! "

Arguments like this have raged down the ages, though at the time Frank Reynolds penned this cartoon for *Punch* he would have had a greater number of little models from which to work in the streets and parks than his modern counterpart. Many youngsters of the 1970s seem to find football or skateboarding satisfying all year round. One thing has remained constant, however: the boy owning the bat and ball commands certain advantages

Girls, probably in their lunch-break and possibly dreaming of their heart-throbs – Hutchings or Woolley or Mason – do their honourable best in the grounds of a factory at Bournville – almost certainly Cadburys – in 1909. Women's cricket still had a long way to go before justifying and establishing itself

The most famous and popular figure at county cricket grounds *outside* the boundary was Yorkshire-born Albert Craig, who frequented The Oval and other grounds, and became known as The Surrey Poet. His penny rhymes extolled all the major players of his time, but never made him rich. When he died in 1909 he went to a pauper's grave at Nunhead, though he had had the pleasure of a get-well note from the Prince of Wales before he drew his last breath. His verses were simple but appealing, and worth a lot to collectors today. His oral wit and ability to silence loud cynics were his greatest attributes, and have never been replaced. He was indeed the 'Captain of the Crowd'

For some devotees the cricket season never ends. Here a game is played on ice in midwinter at Sheffield Park, Sussex, seat of the Earl of Sheffield (who financed an English team, led by Grace, to Australia in 1891–92 and was the instigator of the Sheffield Shield). In warmer weather His Lordship entertained teams from overseas, greeting them with spectacular firework displays

In June 1914 the centenary of Lord's Ground was celebrated with a match between the MCC side which had toured South Africa during the previous winter and a Rest of England team, who won by an innings (Humphreys 111, Hitch 12 for 93). Three kings stand in front of the pavilion: George V (talking to the sturdy 40-year-old C. B. Fry, with Lord Hawke facing J. W. H. T. Douglas), Prince Albert (later George VI) with cane, and the Prince of Wales (later Edward VIII). At a dinner at the Hotel Cecil that evening Lord Hawke expressed a conviction that Lord's and the MCC would continue to flourish no matter what kind of world it would be a hundred years hence. *Below:* Street cricket continues on its crude and merry way despite obstacles

The recent decision of the Police Commissioner to allow no more Cricket in the London Streets has seriously affected the position of the Took's Court Eleven.   It was a very *Crack* Team—see Windows

These serious, uniformed females are the Original English Lady Cricketers, one of two teams, a Red XI and a Blue XI, that travelled the country, playing exhibition matches among themselves and against local women's teams for two years until they were disbanded, the manager apparently disappearing with the profits. The girls, who played under assumed names, were not expected ever to compete against men on equal terms, but *James Lillywhite's Cricketers' Annual* for 1890, from which this picture is taken, granted that 'in time past there has been far too little scope for ladies to indulge in healthful and invigorating exercise, mainly for the reason that "Mrs Grundy" pronounced everything of the kind hoydenish and unladylike'

The Gentlemen v Players match at The Oval, 1906, when W. G. Grace (at point, second from right) played for the amateurs for the last time, turning 58 on the last day, when he scored 74 to ensure a draw. The picture shows Guy Napier, of Cambridge and Middlesex (killed in France while attached to the 35th Sikhs Regiment), bowling to Jim Iremonger, of Notts, a soccer international as well as a stalwart county cricketer. *Left:* Arthur Haygarth, an eminent example of a man who fails to make a mark as a player – he was a deadly dull batsman for Harrow School, MCC, the Gentlemen and other sides – but who makes a memorable contribution to the game in another way. Haygarth, who died in 1903, aged 77, devoted his lifetime, and considerable expenditure, to compiling the invaluable *Cricket Scores and Biographies*, 14 volumes of immensely detailed work for which cricket students will forever remain indebted

It would always have been a comfort to parents to know that their children were engaged in nothing more dangerous than a 'Test match' in the park. Lucien Davis's woodcut, entitled 'Our National Game', depicts some late-Victorian youngsters intent on proving themselves under the scrutiny of elders probably reflecting on their own days of carefree abandon. *Below:* Britain ruled the waves, but 'tip-and-run' deck cricket (here on HMS *Irresistible*) served as an aid to fitness and morale. As the Empire grew so cricket was among the English products taken to every shore visited by Her Majesty's battleships and merchantmen

At The Oval in July 1914 the second-last Gentlemen v Players match before the war gets under way – the last was played at Lord's the following week – and on a damp wicket the professionals lose three for 12 before Gunn and Woolley, and later Hitch and Strudwick, raise a score that, with Hobbs's second-innings century, ensures a handsome victory. Here, Warner catches Hearne off Surrey left-arm bowler Kirk. The wicketkeeper is D. C. Robinson of Gloucestershire. *Below:* The curious designations Married Men's XI and Single Ladies' XI served to bring together these citizens of Whitby, Yorkshire in 1892. Might the topee worn by the girls on the left be precursors of the protective helmets which are becoming such a common sight in 1978?

BENETFINK'S

The Great City Depot for all CRICKET REQUISITES.

CRICKET SHIRTS.

	Boys'.	Men's.
White Oxford Matt	1/9, 3/- ...	1/11, 3/6, 4 6
White Duck	2/3	2/6
Flannel	3/-, 4/- ...	3/3, 4/6, 5/11, 6/11
Fine White Twill ("The County")		4 11

UMPIRES' COATS.

4/11, 6/6, 8/6, 10/6.

Postage free.

CRICKET BALLS.

Duke's SUPER .	... 5/3
Dark's CROWN ..	... 5/-
Wis len's CROWN	... 5/-
GRA=SHOPPER ...	... 5/-
Benetfin\'s PRACTICE, 3-seam	... 3/6
Do , B.C.B. warranted	4/6
Do., do. Boy's ...	. 3 1
Wisden's SPECIAL SCHOOL Boys'	...3/10

Postage free.

CRICKET CAPS.

No. 7. Flannel (*as Illustration*).

Three Colour Stripes, Silk lined, 6 different designs in stock, 1/6 each, 16 6 per doz.

Two Colour Stripes, ¾ in., any 2 colours, from 1/- each, or 10/6 per doz.

Plain Colour Caps with Three-Letter Silk Mo gram, 1/9 each, or 18/- per doz.

Postage free.

CRICKET TROUSERS.

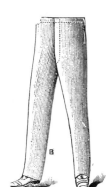

White Flannel Shrunk (Boys')	4/6, 5/6, 7/
Ditto (Men's),	4/11, 5/11, 7/11
Boys' White Flannel Knickers ...	3/3, 4/3

Men's.
Best Quality Flannel, well shrunk ...	9/11
Best White Doe Cloth, guaranteed London shrunk	15/6
Plain Grey or Striped Flannel ...	7/6, 10/6
White Drill	5/11, 7/6

Postage free.

CRICKET BOOTS.

Men's.

The "UNIVERSAL," White Canvas, Leather, or Red Rubber Sole 4/11

The "SPECIAL," White Mock Buck, Spiked, equal in wear and appearance to real Buck (*as Illustration*) 8/11

The "MARYLEBONE," Buck Dressed, Pyramid Spikes, real Buck Toe Cap, round or square toes 10/6

The "LORDS." Real Buck Skin, Guaranteed Machine Welted, equal to Hand Sewn, Pyramid Spikes... ... ...   16 6

Postage free.

CRICKET BLAZERS.

To match No. 7 Cap, as above, 9/11 each.

CRICKET STUMPS.

	Boys.
Polished Ash, 26-in.	1/6
Ditto, 28-in. ...	1 11
Brass Ferrules, 26-in. ...	2/4
Ditto, 28-in. ...	2/6

	Men's.
Polished Ash	2/6
Brass Ferrules (*as Illustration*)	3/-
Ditto, Steel Shod... ...	4 -

Postage, 7d.

Solid Brass Tops	5/3
Ditto. Steel Shod	6/6
Ditto, Revolving Tops ...	7/-
Ditto, Steel Shod ...	8 -

Postage free.

BENETFINK & CO., 107 & 108, CHEAPSIDE, LONDON, E.C

What the well-equipped cricketer was wearing in 1906. A flannel shirt for six-and-eleven, best white doe cloth trousers for fifteen-and-six, 'Lord's' buckskin boots for sixteen-and-six, monogrammed cap for one-and-nine, and – naturally – a matching blazer (a penny change from ten bob). For about £2/10/0 a man could be the answer to a maiden's – if not necessarily his captain's – prayer

Lord's in 1909, with the players taking refreshment and the onlookers performing the traditional promenade, renewing acquaintances, comparing fashions, or simply taking satisfaction from treading the field, so recently trodden by the flannelled gods. The grandstand was replaced in 1930 and in 1958 the Warner Stand filled the space to the left

This family dressed for the occasion – the Eton–Harrow match at Lord's in 1909. Breakfast may have been rushed and the females may have worked up a frenzy as they sorted through their wardrobes, but this day was to be approached as no ordinary, casual day

That cricket has never become Scotland's national game is hardly the fault of such cricketers as James Allan, who was enthusiastic and evangelistic in approach. He was one of the finest batsmen in Scotland up to 1890, and a driving force in the Western Cricket Union. He conceived the idea of a cricket match on a frozen Loch Lomond, but even that imaginative piece of marketing failed to capture the collective Scots interest. *Below:* Any survivors from this group of juvenile park cricketers and spectators will be approaching ninety now, their tension and delight long since washed away by the years

It was not always all sunlight and warmth in the Golden Age, but these gentlemen at the Oxford-and-Cambridge match at Lord's in 1907 came prepared, and partook of their picnic while the rain pattered against their umbrellas. That evening, over a brandy and cigar at the club, they doubtless debated Napier's and Morcom's destruction of Oxford and Sussex's humiliation of the touring South Africans for 49 all out at Brighton the same day

Not a banner in sight, nor a beer-can or bare torso. Just a cross-section of working-class and middle-class Londoners enjoying the Test match against Australia at The Oval in August 1909. For their money they saw left-hander Warren Bardsley reach his second hundred of the match, Victor Trumper stumped for 20 in his final Test innings in England, and a half-century from Wilfred Rhodes as the match drifted to a draw. *Below:* A morsel of 'muscular Christianity' as the small boys of a prep school, far from the roar of the crowds, have time-honoured principles of technique and morality instilled into them

PREPARING FOR A MATCH

THE GARDENERS

THE LAMPOSTS
MAKE GOOD
WICKETS.

BACK PLAY

TIP AND RUN

Parentless boys seeking pleasure from improvised cricket at the Foundling Hospital at Guilford Street, Coram's Fields, London – as a *Daily Graphic* artist saw it in 1905

When costers were seen playing cricket in a London park in the summer of 1904 the *Daily Graphic* wondered if next they would give up shovehap'ny for bridge!

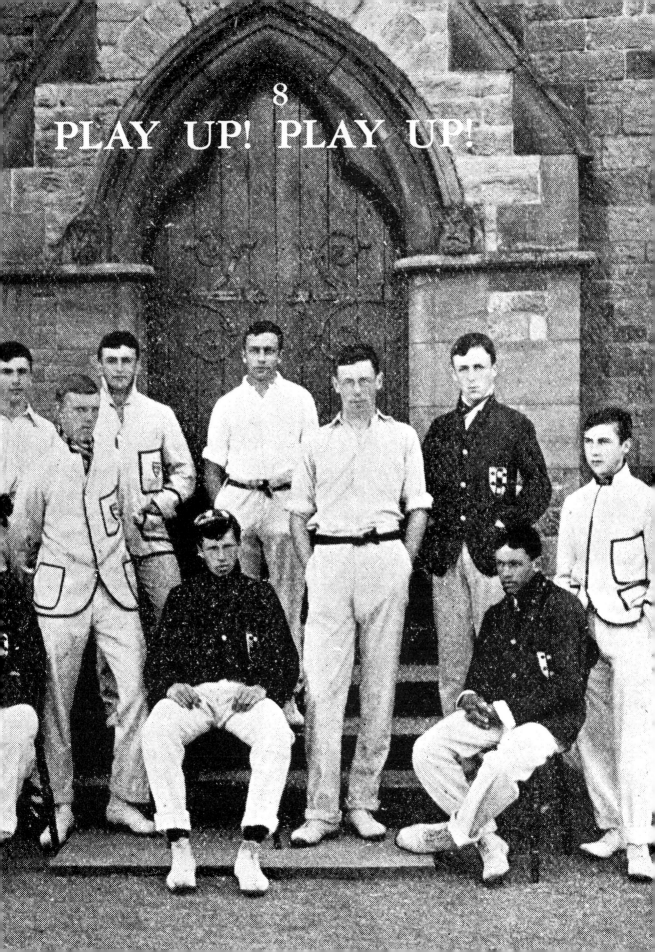

8
PLAY UP! PLAY UP!

Few school teams of any era could have held their own against the Repton XI of 1908, six of whom were invited to play for their respective counties in the August holidays (two had to decline). Standing – I. P. F. Campbell, J. L. S. Vidler, A. T. Sharp, D. FitzGibbon; seated – A. E. Cardew, W. T. Greswell, H. S. Altham (captain), C. E. Squire, R. Sale; front – D. W. Ellis, W. B. Franklin. Harry Altham gave much during a lifetime in cricket and schoolteaching. An Oxford Blue, he played for Surrey and Hampshire, won a DSO and MC in the Great War, and later wrote *A History of Cricket*, one of the most reliable of volumes. A Test selector, MCC treasurer and 1959 president, he was never happier than when coaching and encouraging schoolboys. The committee suite at the MCC Indoor School at Lord's has been named in his memory

Some faces soon to become very famous look out from the Trinity College, Cambridge XI of 1893: standing – R. A. Studd, K. S. Ranjitsinhji, R. C. Norman, W. G. Druce, E. Field; seated – C. M. Wells, C. G. Pope, A. R. Hoare, F. S. Jackson, M. G. Tollemache; front – T. T. Phelps. *Below:* Less auspicious – the Granby Road Board School cricket team, Leicester, 1901, with Fred Root, in brown pads, clutching bat, a future England fast-medium inswing bowler, and Fred Osborn, behind the stumps, who played a couple of times as an all-rounder for Leicestershire but made more of a name for himself as a footballer

Cricket has been a passion at Harrow School for over a century, and on its playing-field, pictured during the 1890s, have ripened the batting and bowling talents of renowned cricketers such as A. J. Webbe, M. C. Kemp, F. S. Jackson, A. C. MacLaren, E. M. Dowson, M. Falcon, M. C. Bird, G. F. Earle, and G. E. V. Crutchley – all before the Great War – with many fine players since upholding the tradition

Cricket at Eton, June 4, 1907, when the college played New College, Oxford. The first Eton v Harrow match was arranged in 1805 by Lord Byron, who scored 7 and 2 in Harrow's innings defeat. In the years leading up to the First World War, Eton produced such outstanding players as C. I. Thornton, Lord Harris, the Studds, the Lytteltons, Bosanquet, the Marshams, R. H. Twining, R. St L. Fowler, and Lord Tennyson. A succession of top-class coaches saw to it that no promise went unnurtured. *Below:* The Eton captain, H. S. Hatfeild, comes in for the luncheon interval under the indulgent admiration of the elders

The Oxford University XI of 1895, every member of which played first-class county cricket, with four going on to play for England: standing – R. P. Lewis, F. H. E. Cunliffe, J. C. Hartley, H. A. Arkwright; seated – F. A. Phillips, H. D. G. Leveson Gower, G. J. Mordaunt (captain), C. B. Fry, H. K. Foster; front – P. F. Warner, G. O. Smith. Despite its unusual strength the side gave best to Cambridge in that year's Varsity match notwithstanding an innings of 121 by Foster. Lewis and Cunliffe were to be killed in action

Merchant Taylors' School, where cricket was at its best around the turn of the century, when J. E. Raphael, J. W. F. Crawford, and T. Dennis were in attendance. When Charterhouse School moved to Godalming the Merchant Taylors' Company acquired the Charterhouse Square site and developed it

Like a muscular chorus-line the Eton XI of 1908 line up for a little pictorial immortality: E. W. S. Foljambe, G. W. Cattley, R. St L. Fowler, L. H. Tennyson, G. H. M. Cartwright, R. L. Benson, R. H. Twining, A. Windsor-Clive, W. A. Worsley, R. O. R. Kenyon-Slaney, F. W. L. Gull

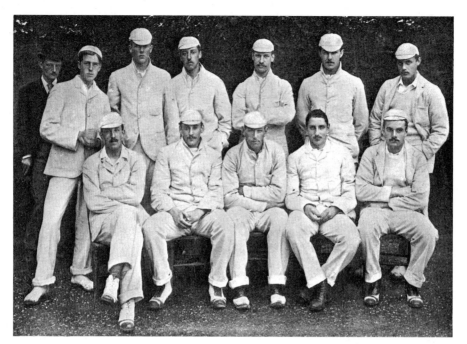

The Cambridge XI of 1890, one of the strongest ever to be fielded by the University. It dismissed Oxford for 42 and 108 to win by seven wickets. Standing – D. L. A. Jephson, E. C. Streatfeild, R. N. Douglas, F. S. Jackson, H. Hale, A. J. L. Hill; seated – C. P. Foley, F. G. J. Ford, S. M. J. Woods (captain), R. C. Gosling, G. MacGregor. Both Woods and Hale were Australian-born

R. H. Spooner (1880–1961), one of the prize products of the Golden Age. Picked for Lancashire a eighteen, fresh from Marlborough College, he scored 44 and 83 against Middlesex at Lord's, with th much-feared Albert Trott among the opposing bowlers. After an interruption through Boer Wa service, his career went from glory to glory, his handsome, wristy strokeplay bringing him double centuries at Trent Bridge, Leyton, Bath, Old Trafford, and The Oval. MacLaren and Spooner wer amateur batsmanship *in excelsis*, and their 368 against Gloucestershire at Liverpool in 1903 remains Lancashire first-wicket record. He played ten times for England, and once at rugby as a centr three-quarter

Vanity Fair drawing by 'Spy

P. F. WARNER

1

A. SHREWSBURY,
NOTTINGHAMSHIRE.

2

J. BRIGGS,
LANCASHIRE.

3

MR. F. S. JACKSON,
YORKSHIRE.

4

R. ABEL,
SURREY.

5

T. RICHARDSON,
SURREY.

6

C. HILL, S.A.

7

MR. K. S. RANJITSINHJI,
SUSSEX.

8

TYLDESLEY

9

A. E. STODDART
MIDDLESEX.

10

J. T. BROWN SENR.,
YORKSHIRE.

11

MR. A. C. MACLAREN (LANCS.).

12

PERSONALITIES OF THE GOLDEN AGE

1. **P. F. Warner**, a symbol of Edwardian cricket and the spirit of Lord's. Playing for Rugby, Oxford, Middlesex, the Gentlemen, and England, he also took the first MCC team to Australia, in 1903–04, and carried the flag to numerous areas within and beyond the Empire. He was knighted in 1937 for his services to cricket and succeeded the Duke of Edinburgh as MCC president in 1950. Despite unreliable health he made 60 centuries, including 132 not out in his first Test

2. **Arthur Shrewsbury**, greatest of professional batsmen in the 1880s and early 1890s. Small, nervous, and reserved, he batted with extraordinary patience, deploying pad-play ahead of its time, but showing mastery of all the strokes. His 164 in the Lord's Test of 1886 was one of cricket's most wonderful performances, lasting seven hours on a dangerous pitch, with Spofforth leading the Australian attack. He was in partnership in business with fellow Notts player Alfred Shaw, and among their enterprises were four tours of Australia, where Shrewsbury captained England in seven Tests. He committed suicide in 1903, aged 47

3. **Johnny Briggs**, still the only man with both a Test century and a Test hat-trick to his name. Notts-born, he served Lancashire through the 1880s and 1890s mainly as a clever slow-medium left-arm bowler and as a right-hand batsman and fine cover fieldsman. Only 5 ft 5 ins, he was of a happy disposition but subject to epileptic fits. He died in Cheadle Asylum in 1902, aged 39

4. **F. S. Jackson**, famed for his successes in the 1905 Tests against Australia, when he won all five tosses, headed the batting, and won the series 2–0. An all-rounder of poise and polish, he had distinguished records at Harrow (where Winston Churchill was his fag) and Cambridge and for Yorkshire and England. No full-time first-class cricketer had so complete a life: he served in the Boer War and the Great War, finishing as Colonel; he was a Unionist MP, Financial Secretary to the War Office, Governor of Bengal, and president of MCC. While in Bengal he escaped five bullets from an assassin, and in his last years he was bombed out and knocked down by a taxi. His style and sense of chivalry on the cricket field were bywords

5. **Bobby Abel**, the small Surrey and England batsman with a large appetite for runs. His unbeaten 357 against Somerset at his beloved Oval in 1899 remains a record for the county, as does his fourth-wicket stand of 448 with Hayward. From 1894 to 1902 he passed 2000 runs each season, not always displaying a straight bat – or the confidence to get behind every ball. Sometimes in need of glasses, he was a favourite of the crowds, and among his distinctions was the fact that he was the first to carry his bat through an England innings

6. **Tom Richardson**, the lion-hearted king of fast bowlers. His reserves of strength, his willingness, and his terrifying pace, cut and bounce were legend. In four seasons (1894–97) he took a phenomenal 1005 wickets in English cricket, despite the larger ball, smaller stumps, narrower crease, and absence of any replacement new ball. Surrey and much of England (and Australia) idolised him, and the Gentlemen-Players match at The Oval was suspended on the afternoon of his funeral in 1912

7. **Clem Hill**, from South Australia, one of the game's most talented left-handers. He made 360 (retired) in a school match in 1893, and first

continued next page

played for Australia in 1896 when only 19. Successive scores of 99, 98, and 97 in the 1901–02 series kept his total of Test centuries down to seven, but his final aggregate of 3412 runs was the best for Australia at the time, and his 365 not out against New South Wales was a Sheffield Shield record until Ponsford beat it. The highlight of Hill's term as a Test selector was a fist fight with colleague Peter McAlister

8. Kumar Shri Ranjitsinhji, the lithe Indian prince who bewitched spectators and fellow-players alike with his magical powers of batsmanship. At Cambridge he hired some prominent English professional fast bowlers to bowl to him in the nets, and by the mid-1890s he was being proclaimed a genius. He made centuries in his first Test against Australia in both countries, and in 1899 he became the first to score 3000 runs in a season. With superlative timing and enchanting wristiness he played every known stroke and introduced the leg-glide besides. His 72 hundreds included 14 double-centuries. In the Great War he was ADC to Sir John French and was mentioned in dispatches. His generosity in later life knew few bounds

9. Johnny Tyldesley, Lancashire's diminutive batting artist of the 1900s. He made 86 centuries, using nimble footwork, blending eager initiative with caution. Wet wickets brought out the best in him, and probably even more commendable than any of his four Test centuries was a 62 at Melbourne on a bad wicket in the 1903–04 rubber. The highest of his 13 double-centuries was 295 not out against Kent in 1906, at Old Trafford

10. A. E. Stoddart, captain of England at cricket and rugby, once holder of the world record score in any class of cricket (485 for Hampstead in an 1886 club match). While leading England in the 1894–95 tour of Australia he made 173 at Melbourne – the highest by an England captain in Australia until 1975 – and in his final match for Middlesex, in 1900, he scored 221. He shared many grand opening partnerships with W. G. Grace, and was the doyen of Lord's. He shot himself in 1915, soon after his 52nd birthday

11. J. T. Brown, scorer of the fastest Test fifty of all time, during his matchwinning century for England at Melbourne in 1895. Stocky and rugged, excelling for a time at the pull stroke, he and John Tunnicliffe had opening stands for Yorkshire of 378 and a then-record 554 before the turn of the century. He made 167 for the Players at Lord's in 1900 when they achieved a remarkable victory over the Gentlemen when set 501 to win. He died of heart failure in 1904, aged only 35

12. Archie MacLaren, whose 424 remains the highest first-class score made by an Englishman. Captain of Harrow, Lancashire and England (22 times, winning only four, losing 11), he made five centuries against Australia, and always assumed the crease with a regal air. To Cardus, the game's most romantic scribe, he was 'very lordly, a man born to rule, to dictate, and to wear the imperial robe'. A blue-riband spectacle of his era was a MacLaren–Fry partnership, as when they put on 309 undefeated for the Gentlemen at Lord's in 1903

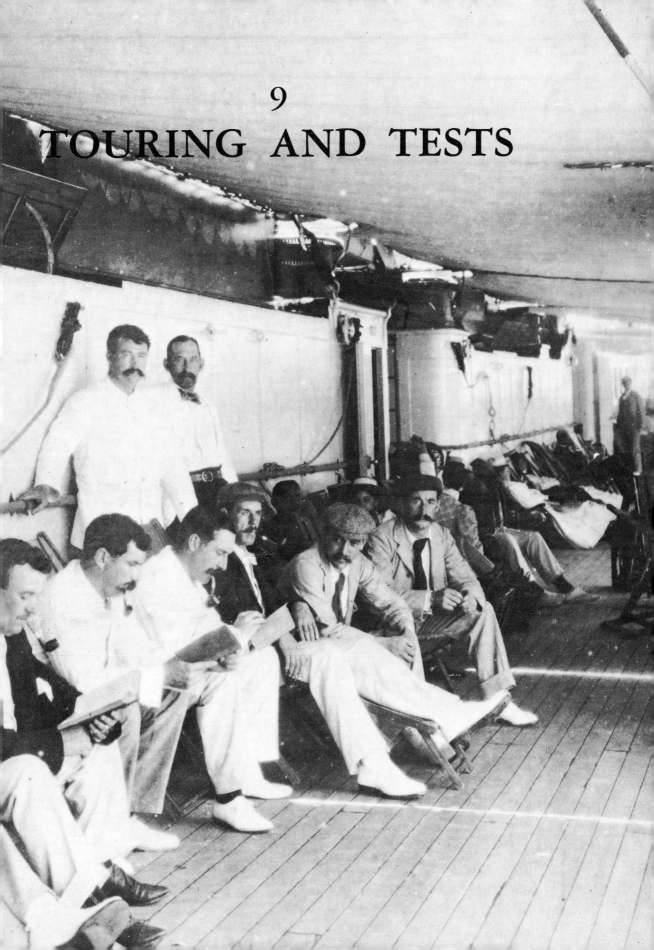

9
TOURING AND TESTS

Lord Hawke's all-amateur 'eat, drink and be merry' tour of North America late in 1891 was broken by a visit to Niagara Falls, where they marvelled at the rashness of Captain Webb, who drowned while trying to cross the rapids eight years earlier

Members of the 1909 Australian touring team inspect Ayres' Kachaball fielding machine at Oxford. Victor Trumper stands second from the left and Charlie Macartney is the smaller figure with hands in blazer pockets. *Below:* Walter Humphreys, the Sussex underarm lob bowler, bowls during Stoddart's English XI's match against Victoria at the Melbourne Cricket Ground in November 1894. Stoddart is at mid-off, Briggs at cover, and the wicketkeeper is L. H. Gay. Bob McLeod faces Humphreys, with Jack Harry the non-striker. Archie MacLaren's 228 in the English XI's first innings was described as probably the best innings ever played on the Melbourne ground

Lunchtime during a Test match at The Wanderers Ground, Johannesburg. The ground was eventually built upon, and now supports the city's main railway station. *Left:* Herby Taylor, one of the best of South African batsmen from any generation. Captain of his country at 24, he put up astonishingly capable resistance against the mighty S. F. Barnes in the 1913–14 series, when that bowler picked off wickets as if on a pigeon-shoot. Taylor went on to make seven Test centuries against England, six of them on his home pitches. He died in 1973, aged 83

Emphasising again the pleasure to be had from starting a cricket tour with a leisurely sea voyage, stopping at places as fascinating as Naples, where the 1909 Australians visited the ruins of Pompeii. Pictured are (from left): Charlie Macartney, Victor Trumper, guide, Bill Whitty, Vernon Ransford, Jack O'Connor, and Hanson Carter

Joe Darling throws in from third man during the Australians' match against Essex at Leyton early in the 1896 tour. *Below:* The Philadelphians who toured England in 1897, well equipped against sunstroke. Back row – J. B. King, H. L. Clark, F. H. Bohlen, M. C. Work (manager), H. C. Thayer, C. Coates; seated – P. H. Clark, E. M. Cregar, G. S. Patterson (captain), F. W. Ralston, A. M. Wood; front – L. Biddle, J. A. Lester, H. B. Baily, F. H. Bates. They lost nine and drew four matches, but beat Sussex (Ranji bowled first ball by King) and Warwickshire

'Big Dave' Nourse, whose son Dudley was to rise to even greater cricket prominence, bowls, cap on, in the South Africa–Australia Test match at Old Trafford during the 1912 Triangular Tournament. The batsman is Claude Jennings, one of those who probably owed their selection to the withdrawal of six of Australia's top players after a dispute with the Board of Control

Breakfast at the hotel for the Australian cricketers early in their tour of England in 1899.
Victor Trumper is nearest the camera, with Jack Worrall at the far end, and the row facing
comprising Bill Howell, Frank Laver, Ernie Jones, and Joe Darling, the captain. Within a
few days Howell was to take all ten Surrey wickets for 28 on his English first-class debut.
Australia's 1897–98 resurgence was sustained by a 1-0 victory in the five-Test series.
Below: Off to the match 1899-style, with a prayer from those on top that it will not rain

Australian wicketkeeper Jim Kelly reclines while Syd Gregory catches up on his correspondence during the early days of the 1899 tour of England. The team were enjoying the comforts of the Inns of Court Hotel, Holborn, London

Hugh Trumble, Australia's tall champion bowler, who often gave the impression of being preoccupied, must have stayed in many a hotel and written many an interesting letter home during his five tours of England. This picture was taken before the team set off for Leyton, where they were to be beaten by Essex by 126 runs. It was no fault of Trumble's. He took 8 for 79 and 4 for 52

Arthur Priestley's team in West Indies in the winter of 1896–97 proved exceedingly popular visitors, and the attractive cricket of Andrew Stoddart, who recorded over 1000 runs and 100 wickets and scored a century on every island, had the locals calling for 'Stoddy' wherever he went. Players pictured (at Bridgetown) are: standing – C. A. Beldam, F. W. Bush, R. Leigh-Barratt, R. P. Lewis, S. M. J. Woods, White (umpire); seated – R. C. N. Palairet, A. E. Stoddart, A. Priestley, W. Williams; front – C. C. Stone, H. T. Stanley. The name Packer appears on the scoreboard eighty years ahead of its time!

Australian giant Warwick Armstrong (second from right) seems especially impressed by King Edward's prize bull as it is paraded for the team at Windsor Castle in 1909. *Below:* Play in progress at Bristol during the Australians' match against Gloucestershire in July 1909

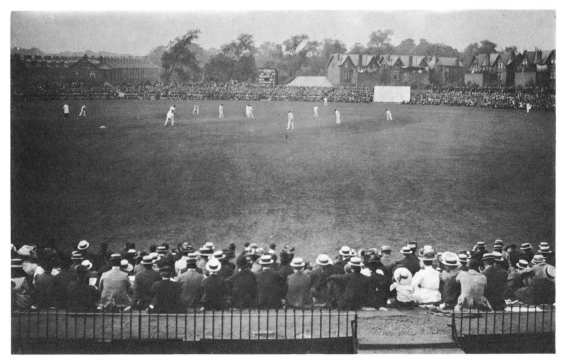

Not a bare head to be seen as spectators stroll round The Oval after England had been dismissed for 352 in reply to Australia's 325 in the 1909 Test match, which was eventually drawn. *Left:* In recent years it has been a rare and expensive privilege for a cricketer to be able to take his wife on a Test tour with him. In earlier years, however, some of the amateurs preferred to be accompanied by their spouses, and 'Plum' Warner, having had the pleasure of the company of his fiancée, Agnes, during the 1903–04 tour of Australia, married her in the following summer

The England XI at Lord's in 1893 was one of the finest ever to take the field. Although Stoddart was captain, thus emulating A. N. Hornby in leading England at rugby and cricket, it seemed no photograph was complete without W. G. Grace, who missed the match because of a broken finger. Standing – E. Wainwright, A. Mold, W. Gunn, J. M. Read; seated – R. Peel, A. E. Stoddart, W. G. Grace, W. H. Lockwood, A. Shrewsbury; front – G. Mac-Gregor, F. S. Jackson, W. Flowers. The match, played on a Monday, Tuesday, and Wednesday, was drawn, Shrewsbury making 106 and Jackson (in his first Test) 91. For Australia, Harry Graham, aged only 22, made a courageous century, the first part of a unique double as he made another in his initial Test innings in Australia 18 months later. His was a sad end: he died in a Dunedin asylum at the age of 40

The 1910–11 series played by South Africa in Australia was won 4-1 by the home side but sterling deeds were performed by players from both teams, seen here in Sydney. Insets – T. Campbell, A. E. E. Vogler; back row – W. Bardsley, S. J. Pegler, C. Kelleway, C. B. Llewellyn, V. S. Ransford, C. O. C. Pearse; second row – W. W. Armstrong, A. W. Nourse, H. V. Hordern, L. A. Stricker, D. R. A. Gehrs, A. Cotter; seated – J. H. Sinclair, V. T. Trumper, P. W. Sherwell (South African captain), C. Hill (Australian captain), R. O. Schwarz, W. J. Whitty, G. A. Faulkner; front – S. J. Snooke, C. G. Macartney, J. M. M. Commaille, H. Carter, J. W. Zulch

Victor Trumper (1877–1915), still considered by thoughtful judges of cricket to have been the greatest of batsmen in that he seemed to have two or three answers to any ball, and often got out through charming negligence. He made tall scores: a triple-century and several double-centuries in Sydney grade cricket, and 300 not out against Sussex in 1899 during his first tour with the Australians. His six other first-class double-centuries included a most beautiful and breathtaking 214 not out against South Africa, and his 185 not out against England at Sydney in 1903–04 was near-perfect. But so often he gave his wicket to a deserving bowler – never ostentatiously – when he had his hundred. There were, he used to say, other fellows who'd like a knock. He was at his most remarkable best on difficult pitches, when his sure touch demonstrated even more forcibly what a disparity there was between his play and that of other batsmen. Shy, lovable, modest to a fault, he died in his 38th year, some months after A. E. Stoddart and some months before W. G. Grace, in 1915, one of cricket's saddest years

Drawing by A. Chevallier Tayler

MR. C.B. FRY,
SUSSEX.

1

C. BLYTHE (KENT).

2

W.H. LOCKWOOD.
SURREY.

3

B.J.T. BOSANQUET

4

R.E. FOSTER

5

W. RHODES,
YORKSHIRE.

6

MR. K.L. HUTCHINGS (KENT).

7

E.G. MACARTNEY, N.S.W.

8

G. GUNN (NOTTINGHAMSHIRE).

9

S.F. BARNES (STAFFORDSHIRE).

10

J.B. HOBBS (SURREY).

11

LILLEY

12

PERSONALITIES OF THE GOLDEN AGE

1. **C. B. Fry**, whose assorted accomplishments would have filled several average lives. Cricketer, athlete, footballer (both codes), scholar, schoolmaster, journalist, naval officer, novelist, he set a record of six successive first-class centuries in 1901, and made 94 in a career during which he played for Oxford, Surrey (once), Sussex, Hampshire, the Gentlemen and England. His partnerships with Joe Vine for the first wicket and with Ranjitsinhji made Sussex a huge attraction

2. **Colin Blythe**, one of the greatest of slow left-arm bowlers, who gave the ball a lot of spin and knew the art of pace-change to near-perfection. A Cockney, he had his best season in 1909, taking 215 wickets at 14, two years earlier having taken 10 for 30 and 7 for 18 in a day at Northampton. A high-class violinist, his sensitivity and proneness to epileptic fits reduced his capacity at times, as when his 15 wickets against South Africa at Leeds in 1907 and 11 against Australia at Birmingham in 1909 left him utterly exhausted. He was killed in action near Ypres in 1917, when aged 38

3. **Bill Lockwood**, immortalised with his Surrey and England partner Richardson among the greatest of fast-bowling duos. Handicapped by an uneven temperament, still on his day he created the impression that no finer fast bowler could ever have lived. He was a good batsman besides, making 15 centuries; but his bowling, especially his vicious breakback and mystifying slower ball, are features of his play best remembered

4. **B. J. T. Bosanquet**, of Eton, Oxford, and Middlesex, who gave cricket a revolutionary manoeuvre – the 'googly' or 'Bosie' or 'wrong 'un', the ball bowled with a leg-break action but which turned the other way because the wrist

was dropped. This ball, delivered in its early days with a marked lack of accuracy, was developed over the years firstly by a South African school and later in England and Australia (the first country to be tormented by it). His best Test analysis was 8 for 107 against Australia at Trent Bridge in 1905, and he was a good enough batsman to make a double-century in a representative match at The Oval in 1908. He also dabbled at billiards, ice-hockey, and the hammer-throw

5. **R. E. Foster**, whose 287 in his first Test match (v Australia, Sydney, 1903–04) remains a record for a debut score. He was the only one of seven Worcestershire brothers to play for England, whom he captained against South Africa in 1907. An exquisite stylist, he mounted all the strokes on a sound defence, and once hit W. G. Grace for four consecutive sixes. He was a brilliant slip fieldsman, and as well as playing for Oxford at cricket, football, rackets, and golf, he played football for England. He died from diabetes in 1914, at the age of 36

6. **Wilfred Rhodes**, who, during a career stretching from 1898 to 1930, recorded almost 40,000 runs and an unrivalled total of 4187 wickets with slow left-arm cunning. He rose from number 11 to opening batsman for England, and still shares the records for the first (323) and last (130) wickets against Australia. He did the 'double' 16 times and gathered 100 wickets in 23 seasons, both unmatched performances. He became a Yorkshire institution, the epitomy of reliability and shrewdness. He died in 1973, aged 95, having been blind for the last few years

7. **Kenneth Hutchings**, one of the most widely mourned casualties of the Great War. An outstanding schoolboy batsman at Tonbridge, he

continued next page

had one exceptional year with Kent, in 1906, when he helped prominently towards their Championship. He was a glorious driver of the ball, exciting spectators by his daring; defence, for him, meant reluctant withdrawal to within the crease area. He made a century for England at Melbourne in 1907–08, but may be considered one of those whose overall records fell short of expectation

8. Charles Macartney, an Australian batsman of near-genius, who made an early name as a slow left-arm bowler. His career spanned the Edwardian years and ended in the late 1920s. In 1921 he scored 345 against Nottinghamshire, and on the next tour, when 40, he made three successive Test centuries. Small and compact, with strong wrists and audacious outlook, he became known as 'The Governor-General'. No batsman ever had more belief in himself. He took 11 for 85 in the 1909 Leeds Test

9. George Gunn, another bold batsman, although a professional. A man of caprice, he sometimes blocked innocent balls because it pleased him, and sometimes went down the wicket to even the fastest bowling and did with it as he liked. When in Australia for his health in 1907 he was called into the England team and made 119 and 74 in his first Test. He made 62 centuries (55 for Notts) and played the last of his 15 Tests in West Indies in 1930, when aged 50

10. S. F. Barnes, considered almost universally to have been the best bowler of them all. In only 26 Test matches he took 189 wickets at 16.43, including 8 for 56 and 9 for 103 at Johannesburg in 1913–14, when aged 40. Bowling fast or medium-pace, with a high arm, spinning the ball either way and generating lift from the pitch, he played comparatively little first-class cricket, preferring to play for Staffordshire and in various leagues, taking all ten wickets in an innings on seven occasions. MacLaren took him to Australia as an almost unknown player in 1901. Ten years later his most renowned spell was bowled at Melbourne, where he dismissed five top Australian batsmen for six runs at the start of the innings. He died in 1967, in his 95th year

11. Jack Hobbs, whose magnificent batting before the Great War tends to be overshadowed by his great deeds for Surrey and England during the 1920s. Yet the younger Hobbs made 65 centuries, many in dashing style, before the war. His final tally of 197 hundreds and his aggregate of 61,237 runs remain unmatched. A modest, popular cricketer, he became a national hero, a complete credit to the game, his career linking those of other supremes in their ages: Grace (against whom he played in his first match for Surrey, in 1905) and Bradman. His prolific partnerships for Surrey's first wicket with Hayward were succeeded through another generation with Sandham (and with Sutcliffe for England), and his contribution did not end with the bat, for he was a superb cover fieldsman. He was the first professional to be knighted. He died in 1963, days after his 81st birthday

12. A. F. A. 'Dick' Lilley, England's wicket-keeper in 35 Test matches between 1896 and 1909, effecting a then-record 92 dismissals. In a long career he took 523 catches and made 132 stumpings for Warwickshire – a strictly old-time ratio – and 899 dismissals in all first-class cricket. A highly-respected professional, he was a sound batsman, making 16 centuries. He first played cricket while working for Cadburys

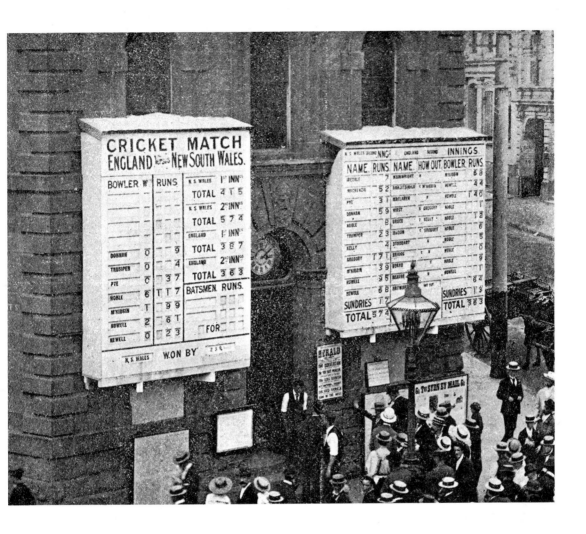

Before radio and television put the sporting world on a network of instant information one device was the progressive scoreboard outside newspaper offices, in this instance the *Herald* and *Mail* in Sydney, during the Englishmen's defeat by New South Wales in February 1898. In six days' play a total of 1739 runs was scored, keeping the operators as well as the bowlers fully occupied

'Tibby' Cotter opens the 1905 Australians' match against the Gentlemen of England at Lord's, with P. F. Warner facing and C. B. Fry the non-striker. For the touring team, fresh from hearing Melba sing in *La Traviata* at Covent Garden, Percy Newland stands up at the stumps, which suggests a below-pace or unusually accurate Cotter, a benign pitch, or all three. The Australians won by an innings after Armstrong had hit 248 not out, Darling 117 not out, and Duff 94, and the Gentlemen collapsed for 66 in the second innings. *Below:* C. B. Fry (in overcoat), England's captain at Leeds against South Africa in 1912, has just been out with the rulebook to persuade the umpire to lift the bails at 1.30 pm. The young trees at the far end of the Headingley ground today stand tall and proud

The seventh Australian team (excluding the 1868 Aborigines) to tour England, who had a tough time of it in 1890, losing two Tests and drawing the other, and losing fourteen other first-class matches. Back row – H. Trumble, J. McC. Blackham, K. E. Burn, Dr J. E. Barrett, H. F. Boyle (manager); seated – F. H. Walters, G. H. S. Trott, W. L. Murdoch (captain), J. J. Lyons, C. T. B. Turner; front – S. E. Gregory, J. J. Ferris, P. C. Charlton, S. P. Jones. The situation regarding Burn, a Tasmanian, was ludicrous. Selected as deputy wicketkeeper, he confessed during the voyage across that he had never kept wicket in his life!

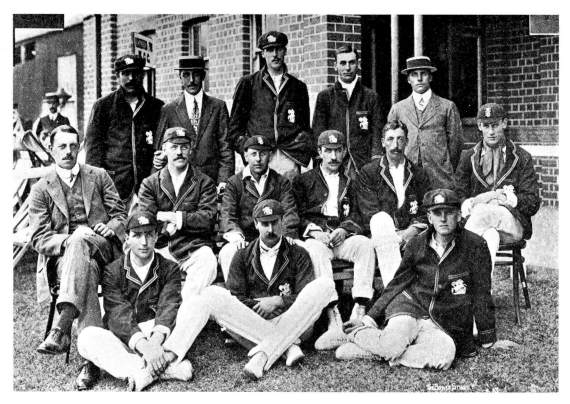

The sixth (1909–10) English team to tour South Africa, pictured in their glamorous MCC blazers at Durban. Back row – G. J. Thompson, W. Rhodes, F. E. Woolley, J. B. Hobbs, H. Strudwick; seated – G. H. Simpson-Hayward, Capt. E. G. Wynyard, H. D. G. Leveson Gower (captain), D. Denton, C. P. Buckenham, M. C. Bird; front – N. C. Tufnell, F. L. Fane, C. Blythe. In spite of the handful of top-class players, England lost the series 2-3, with Faulkner achieving wonders with bat and ball for South Africa and Vogler taking 36 wickets with leg-breaks and googlies

Sunday morning breakfast upstairs for Australian cricketers Algie Gehrs, Bert Hopkins, and Reg Duff at Christchurch during the visit to New Zealand on the way to England in 1905

Hardly resembling the typical Australian tourist, M. A. Noble feeds the pigeons in Venice en route to England with the 1899 team. The stench in this watery Italian city was 'unbearable', according to Frank Laver, the diarist among the players. *Below:* Going the other way – when *Ormuz*, taking Stoddart's second team to Australia in 1897, berthed at Port Said, the huge figure of Tom Richardson turned heads as it strode past Simon Arzt, the store known to so many Suez passengers over the years

A 'mini-Test' in a square, probably in London, during the Australians' 1905 tour. The bowler is Syd Gregory, while the toddler is encircled by Joe Darling (wicketkeeper), Algie Gehrs and Jim Kelly, with Mrs Clem Hill in the background. *Below:* S. F. Barnes on a lively wicket at The Oval in England's Test match against South Africa in 1912 was not only a physical threat to the Springboks, but here has injured his own wicketkeeper, 'Tiger' Smith, who had to go off for repairs. England won by ten wickets in two days, Barnes taking 13 for 57

The last MCC team to tour before the Great War: Johnny Douglas's 1913–14 combination, pictured aboard *Saxon* before departure. Thanks chiefly to Barnes, who took 49 wickets (he played in only four of the five Tests), England won 4-0. Perched on the windlass are H. Strudwick, J. W. Hearne, and A. E. Relf; on the rail – M. C. Bird, L. H. Tennyson, and W. Rhodes; on his haunches – J. B. Hobbs; standing – M. W. Booth, F. E. Woolley, S. F. Barnes, and J. W. H. T. Douglas (half-sitting). C. P. Mead is extreme right (in bowler), but the gentleman leaning against the companionway is unidentified. E. J. Smith, Strudwick's deputy as wicketkeeper, is missing from the group

The much-vaunted 1902 Australian touring team, who absorbed dismissal for 36 in the drawn Edgbaston Test to win the series 2-1, two of the finishes being classic thrillers (a three-run win at Old Trafford and a one-wicket loss at The Oval). Back row – W. P. Howell, H. Trumble, Major B. J. Wardill (manager), W. W. Armstrong, A. J. Y. Hopkins, R. A. Duff; seated – V. T. Trumper, M. A. Noble, J. Darling, J. V. Saunders, J. J. Kelly; front – H. Carter, S. E. Gregory. Absent – E. Jones

The Australians often stayed at The Cricketers, Mitcham, run by former England cricketer James Southerton. Here, on the 1896 tour, Clem Hill, Hugh Trumble, and Tom McKibbin emerge for net practice

Another milliner's delight – several thousand Australian heads immune to the discomforts inflicted by sun, wind or rain. All are intent on play in the first Australia–England Test match of 1901–02 from the vantage point of the Sydney Hill. The cycle track was then about five years old, and the view of Paddington Town Hall (top left) and the terraced houses was unimpaired until fairly recently. Progress, in the shape of the Bradman Stand at the far end, has blocked out the Town Hall

The view from the rail of *Orontes* as she sailed from Melbourne in March 1909, with M. A. Noble and his cricketers aboard. Most of them would not be seeing their wives and families for seven or eight months, though among the compensations were new sights daily, and the honour of representing Australia, who retained the Ashes this time two matches to one. *Below:* A modern-looking sweep shot – not by Denis Compton but by Johnny Douglas, Essex captain, in the match against the 1912 Australians at Leyton. The wicketkeeper is Bill Carkeek

Douglas mis-hits in his innings of 60 against the Australians, who replied to Essex's 192 with 564 for 3 declared (Macartney 208, Bardsley 184 not out) and went on to win by an innings. Douglas drowned while trying to save his father after the collision between *Oberon*, the ship on which they were travelling, and *Arcturus* in the Cattegat a week before Christmas 1930. *Below:* Three years earlier, also at Leyton, Victor Trumper played his second-last match in England, and scored 71 against Essex in a dazzling 95 minutes before being caught at slip. Here he makes a rare miscue

Above: Albert Relf bowls to Reginald Hands, of Western Province, at Newlands, Cape Town, during MCC's tour of 1913–14. Both were tragic figures: Relf shot himself in 1937 and Hands died from war wounds in 1918. *Left:* Australian Cricketers Brawl In Main Street – what a headline this would have made! But it was a 'put-up job' to relieve the boredom of the long train journey across America after the 1896 tour of England. To increase the absurdity, little Syd Gregory was matched against lofty Hugh Trumble, neither of them removing his headwear. Deputy wicketkeeper Alf Johns (left) holds the coats while Ernie Jones (right) is keeper of the 'purse'

A flat finish to a distinguished career awaited Syd Gregory, captain of the 1912 Australian touring team, posing in his New South Wales blazer as *Otway* neared the English coast. Born at the Sydney Cricket Ground, where his father was curator, he made his Test debut in 1890, when he was twenty, and in 1894 he made the first Test double-century in Australia. No-one has yet equalled 'Tich' Gregory's record 52 appearances in England – Australia Tests

The 1896 Australians, some of whom could have walked right through the City of London without being identified as 'colonial'. Back row, between umpires – Harry Musgrove (manager), Tom McKibbin; second row – Hugh Trumble, Alf Johns, Harry Graham, Joe Darling; third row – Frank Iredale, Ernie Jones, George Giffen, Charles Eady, Jim Kelly; front – Harry Donnan, Syd Gregory, Harry Trott (captain), Clem Hill. They won 18 and lost four of their 31 first-class matches, and conceded only three centuries altogether, but they lost the Test series 1-2. Only five of the players had toured England previously, but then, as ever since, Australia had the knack of finding talented new cricketers without much difficulty whenever the need arose. A disquieting feature of this tour, however, was that Jones and McKibbin, both of whom took over a hundred wickets, were considered by a number of judges, including the editor of *Wisden*, to have illegal bowling actions. It was thought proper to speak out only after the tour had ended

Above: The MCC players, led off by Albert Knight and wicketkeeper Herbert Strudwick, leave the field at Melbourne during the 1903–04 tour. Rhodes has his sweater over his arm, Arnold is putting his on, and skipper Warner is to the left of the main group. *Right:* Some of the Australians – Hill, Trumble, Kelly and Trumper – make use of some spare hours to inspect Nelson's HMS *Victory* in Portsmouth Harbour. *Below:* Horses, having been all but totally excluded from the streets, remained a while longer to do an efficient and economical job of pulling the roller over the cricket square, as here at Sydney

Above: On an evidently cool day in 1912 Australian left-arm fast bowler Bill Whitty has a net with a well-worn bat and contrasting batting gloves. Whitty, the last survivor of Australia's pre-1914 Test cricketers at the time of his death in 1974 at the age of 87, was a fine bowler, who claimed Trumper's wicket with remarkable regularity in domestic cricket, and had one glorious series when he took 37 wickets against South Africa in 1910–11. *Left:* Jimmy Sinclair, South Africa's powerful all-rounder, and Aubrey Faulkner march out to bat at Lord's during the 1907 tour. Yet again tragedy lurked in the future, for Sinclair died in 1913 at the early age of 36, and Faulkner, after surviving the war, in which he was awarded the DSO, and starting a successful cricket school in London, gassed himself in September 1930

The 1891–92 English team in South Africa was strong enough – even though an even stronger side was touring Australia – to go through its 20 matches undefeated, winning 13 matches including the only Test, at Cape Town, where Harry Wood of Surrey became the first full-time wicketkeeper to score a Test hundred (it was the only century of his first-class career). Back row – J. Leaney (umpire), E. J. Leaney, F. Martin, G. W. Ayres, A. D. Pougher, W. Chatterton, Edwin Ash (manager); seated – H. Wood, G. G. Hearne, J. T. Hearne, W. W. Read (captain), J. J. Ferris, W. L. Murdoch; front – W. Brockwell, G. Brann, V. A. Barton, A. Hearne. The most successful batsman was Chatterton, from Derbyshire, with 951 runs at 41.34, and Ferris headed the bowling figures with 234 wickets at 5.46. A sad sidelight to the solitary Test match was that Transvaaler Clarence Wimble made two ducks in his one and only appearance for South Africa

In the 'Triangular Test' at The Oval between England and South Africa in 1912 the visitors were thrashed by ten wickets in less than two days. Easily the highest South African innings came from 'Big Dave' Nourse, whose 42 was terminated by this caught-and-bowled by Frank Foster. Had he missed the catch there was a fair chance that Nourse's partner would have been run out!

Essex wicketkeeper Jack Freeman (brother of Kent spinner A. P. 'Tich' Freeman) stabs out a foot but fails to stop a leg-glance by Australia's Vernon Ransford off Douglas in the third match of the 1909 tour, at Leyton. Bardsley (219) and Ransford (174) made 355 in 200 minutes for the third wicket, and the tourists eventually won by an innings and 117 runs

They could pass for a school (or whatever the collective term may be) of detectives, but they are merely the amateur members of the MCC team which set out to tour New Zealand at the end of the 1902 summer. From the left: B. J. T. Bosanquet, A. E. Leatham, F. L. Fane, P. R. Johnson, E. M. Dowson, T. L. Taylor, J. N. Tonge, C. J. Burnup, P. F. Warner (captain)

Innocent pleasure for touring Australian cricketers Jack O'Connor and Hanson 'Sammy' Carter at Hastings as the 1909 tour drew to a close. Truly did Maxim Gorky once write, 'In the carriages of the past you can't go anywhere'

10 THE GAME OF WAR

Colin ('Charlie') Blythe, of Kent and England, who took 100 wickets in 19 Tests, and 2506 wickets in all first-class cricket at only 16.81 apiece. He had retired when war broke out, and had accepted a job at Eton College, but his skill was such that Kent would have been glad of his services whenever he might have been available. Despite his epileptic condition, he enlisted in the Kent Fortress Engineers, reaching the rank of sergeant, but was killed in 1917, one of the most deeply mourned of sportsmen. A memorial to Blythe stands at the entrance to the St Lawrence ground, Canterbury, and in the museum there, two shrapnel-riddled wallets, removed from his body, are displayed

This lad, Arthur Edward Jeune Collins, in June 1899, when not quite fourteen, made the highest score recorded – to this day. Batting on five afternoons, he made 628 not out, 501 of them by the second evening, and the balance in playing time much curtailed by rain. His team, Clark's House, beat North Town (61 and 87) by an innings and 685 runs in this junior house match at Clifton College, and Collins overcame any tiredness he may have felt to take 7 for 33 and 4 for 30. Boundary hits on one side of the ground, incidentally, counted only as twos. He hit 146 twos. An 'easy, graceful' batsman, Collins, born in India, had been orphaned in 1898, and joined the Royal Engineers after leaving Clifton. He was posted to India, and played little further cricket in England, though he often showed that he might have succeeded in top-class cricket. It was his misfortune and embarrassment to be reminded of the 628 wherever he played, a pressure which served to emphasise his taciturn nature. On November 11, 1914 Captain 'Boy' Collins, having been married only a few months previously, and mentioned in dispatches in October, was shot and killed in the first Battle of Ypres

Greatness – and greatness that was not to be. Charlie Macartney looks up at another highly talented Australian, Jack Massie, 6 ft 4 in, from New South Wales, whom Johnnie Moyes reckoned the best left-arm bowler he ever saw. Son of old Test captain H. H. Massie, he was a star footballer, oarsman, boxer and athlete, and was probably the best bowler in Australia when war began, but a mutilated foot, courtesy of a German sniper, ended it all

Warwickshire cricketer Percy Jeeves, who gave his name to P. G. Wodehouse's deathless fictional manservant, was one of the most promising all-rounders in England in 1914 – perhaps the best in the land. Yorkshire-born, he was 26, and bowled fast-medium, off an easy action, with a lot of movement. He was well-liked and was expected to play for England in the coming years. But, with thousands of others, he answered the call, wondering, no doubt, when cricket might be played again with an easy mind. For him, the last autumn had closed in. Serving with the Royal Warwickshire Regiment, he was killed in the summer of 1916

One of the most pathetic figures in a heartrending period of history was Percy Frederick Hardy, Dorset-born and an irregular Somerset professional left-hand batsman for ten years before the war. He seldom made the news, but returned some useful performances, including a top score of 91 against Kent at Taunton in 1910 (to which he added the treasured wicket of Woolley, a feat he repeated twice the following season). He was a private in the County of London Yeomanry, oppressed by the thought of going to the Front and, when his wife last spoke with him, comforting himself as best he could with drink. He was found on the morning of March 9, 1916 on the floor of the public lavatory at King's Cross Station with his throat deeply gashed and a bloodstained knife by his side. A verdict of suicide was returned. Hardy's fearful, unfathomable torment was at an end

Albert 'Tibby' Cotter was a wild and furious Australian fast bowler who would give his last ounce of energy on the hottest day. Idolised by the sporting fraternity of Sydney, he enlisted in the Australian Light Horse and was shot at Beersheba when he raised his head above the rim of the trench to verify what his periscope had shown. He was 33

The regal and portly officer photographed by Vandyk of London in 1915 is Prince Ranjitsinhji, maker of so many runs . . . and friends . . . and resolves to improve his people's lot and the Empire's chances of survival in the face of the greatest threat yet

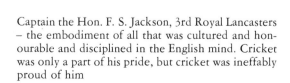

Captain the Hon. F. S. Jackson, 3rd Royal Lancasters – the embodiment of all that was cultured and honourable and disciplined in the English mind. Cricket was only a part of his pride, but cricket was ineffably proud of him

The pavilion at Old Trafford Cricket Ground became a Red Cross hospital during the war, and with beds lining the corridors and landings – and even the roof in fine weather – 1800 patients were treated in the four years. A scarcely credible account later claimed that some members refused to pay their Lancashire County Cricket Club subscriptions during the war years because they felt that some cricket ought to have been played at Old Trafford

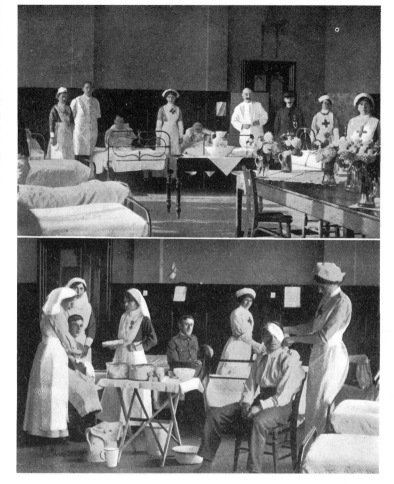

Putting his coins into a Red Cross Fund collection box in 1915 is Dr W. G. Grace, the 'Grand Old Man' himself, his own time fast running out. An age was terminated, a desecration was being inflicted on mankind. The glories and delights of the Golden Age had come to an end

INDEX